LIFE AFTER
BRISTOL ROVERS

The Author

Mark Leesdad has been a Bristol soccer fan for more years than he cares to remember. After spending his early youth watching games at Eastville Stadium and Ashton Gate, he turned to playing and only one thing stopped him making it as a professional – complete lack of skill!

Mark honed his interviewing and writing skills as an editor and press officer with two major companies in Bristol, before embarking on sports writing with a newspaper with the best Sunday sports coverage in the south west, *The Sunday Independent*.

LIFE AFTER
BRISTOL ROVERS

MARK LEESDAD

This book is dedicated to the memory of my sister Linda Thompsett.

First published 2007

Tempus Publishing Limited
The Mill, Brimscombe Port,
Stroud, Gloucestershire, GL5 2QG
www.tempus-publishing.com

Modern photography © Phil McCheyne, 2007

British Library Cataloguing in Publication Data.
A catalogue record for this book is available from the British Library.

ISBN 978 0 7524 4153 5

Typesetting and origination by Tempus Publishing Limited.
Printed in Great Britain.

Contents

Acknowledgements

Where the devil do you start with 'thank yous'? So many people, so little space. To my old office manager Eric Bradford, who inadvertently got me into the writing game, and to two of my old bosses – Christine Foster and Bill Edwardes – who encouraged and supported me, huge 'thank yous'. Also, to another of my old bosses, Richard Smith, who convinced me to get rid of my carrier pigeons and typewriter, and move into the twenty-first century and learn to use a computer (badly), thanks.

Having been brought up to believe that any story is only as good as the accompanying photograph, I owe a debt of gratitude to the photographer I have worked with for a number of years – Phil McCheyne of Nailsea. Phil 'I also do weddings, passport photos, commercial/industrial photography, company presentations, etc' McCheyne has taken practically all of the modern-day photographs of our heroes.

Throughout this book I have endeavoured to ensure non breach of copyright and have not used photographs carrying a copyright stamp without permission. As far as the playing days pictures are concerned, I need to thank various newspapers (credits as shown) which have allowed me to reproduce these photos. And a huge thank you to Bristol Rovers' historian (and fellow sports author) Mike Jay, who has let me use countless photographs from his personal library, the majority of which were taken by Bristol Rovers' official photographer Alan Marshall. Mike has also been a source of tremendous help with biographical details. Bless you Mike.

To the officials and directors at Bristol Rovers, who have bent over backwards to help, my grateful thanks.

I must also thank Tempus Publishing for having the faith in this project to support and produce this book.

Most of all, my eternal and grateful thanks to the many former players featured. Those stars of yesteryear who gave up their time to welcome me into their workplaces and homes to tell me their stories (some of which have not been retold as they are covered by the unofficial players secret act!) and to lend me treasured photographs from their scrapbooks. Without their co-operation this project would have fallen at the first fence.

Finally (at last, you say!) thank YOU for buying this book. I hope reading it gives you as much pleasure as writing it gave me.

Mark Leesdad

Far left: Author Mark Leesdad.

Left: Photographer Phil McCheyne.

Introduction

There was always something mystical and unique about Eastville Stadium. The smell of the gasworks, the dog track going right around the pitch and the flower beds behind the goals. And those pies. They did the most wonderful steak and kidney pies. There was also something magical about Rovers supporters, who have supported their team through thick and thin, and who love nothing more than breaking into a chorus of 'Goodnight Irene' when their side is flying.

And let's not forget the reason for this book. There were also some marvellous players at Bristol Rovers. Alfie 'The Baron' Biggs, Harold Jarman flying down the wing, the late Geoff Bradford... the list is endless, so I'll stop there.

But what became of these heroes of yesteryear? And what about some of the players who didn't reach the dizzy heights of messrs Biggs, Jarman and Bradford? What did they all do after their professional footballing days were over?

In *Life After Bristol Rovers* I've tried to answer those questions, as well as go over their playing careers. The professions they've chosen to go into are varied – driving, pharmacy, bar management, plumbing, recruitment, law and order and, of course, some are still involved in some capacity or other in 'the beautiful game'. Sadly, some that I saw play, like Geoff Bradford, Micky Barrett and Doug Hillard, are no longer with us.

Nostagia; is it all it's cracked up to be? If, like me, you enjoy the odd look back, as well as finding out what those heroes of the soccer pitch did after Rovers, then the answer is yes and this book is for you or one of your loved ones.

PETER AITKEN

It was always on the cards that former Eastville favourite Peter Aitken would end up back at Bristol Rovers. So it comes as no surprise that Peter is a community officer for The Pirates, a position he has held for the past five years. 'I love it,' said Peter. 'I do a lot of work with schools and my patch goes right up to South Gloucestershire, which is a fair old catchment area.'

Peter's love affair with Rovers began in earnest when he signed professional forms in the 1972/73 season. A versatile player, he could perform with ease at full-back, in midfield or as a central defender.

An uncanny ability to turn defence into attack with a timely tackle followed by a precision pass that put his side on the offensive made Peter a firm favourite with Rovers' fans and saw him called up to the Welsh Under-23 side. His career ground to a temporary halt when he broke his leg at Eastville in a game against Nottingham Forest in 1975, but he fought his way back to fitness and went on to captain the Rovers side.

With over 260 senior games under his belt (and four goals), Peter moved across town to play for rivals City, where he played regularly for the next two years before the club went into financial freefall and he became one of the 'Ashton Gate Eight' – the senior players who agreed to leave the club in order to save them from bankruptcy.

After City, Peter had a short spell at York City and an even shorter spell with Bournemouth – one senior game as a non-contract player – before joining the soccer exodus of players trying their luck overseas. 'I had a season playing in Hong Kong, which was very interesting,' he explained. 'There were quite a few ex-pats over there at the time – Tommy Hutchinson, Barry Powell, John Clayton and Barry Daines come to mind – and it was a fascinating experience.'

Looking back on his career, who did he rate as the most skilful forward he has had to face? 'I remember playing for Rovers against Fulham when a certain George Best was playing for them,' replied Peter. 'He was one of my heroes and, like a lot of defenders before me, I spent the match trying to get the ball off him – and failing.'

After Hong Kong, Peter came back to Bristol. He had four years playing for Bath City and also went to work for Rolls Royce at Filton, before getting the call to return to his beloved Rovers, representing the club in the community.

Married to Gillian, the couple have two teenage daughters and live in Stapleton, just a stone's throw from the old Eastville stadium.

Left: Peter (right) in action for Bristol Rovers at Eastville.

Below: Back with Rovers, Peter is now a community officer for the club.

IAN ALEXANDER

When Glasgow-born Ian 'Jock' Alexander made his first senior appearance in the Scottish Football League and set up his team's match-winner, his father was not best pleased:

> Me and dad were Rangers supporters and I'd always dreamed of playing for The Gers. But when I finally did get to play at Ibrox, I was playing for Motherwell and set up the winner AGAINST Rangers. Dad didn't speak to me for a month!

These days the former tough-tackling Rovers full-back works for a company involved in recruitment in the construction industry. The thick dark hair has been replaced with a closer cropped style, and the moustache has long since disappeared – 'My wife said it made me look like a porn star, so it went!' is Ian's explanation.

It was at Rotherham United, managed then by the late Emlyn Hughes, that Ian's football career began. After two years playing in the Second Division with The Merry Millers, he was on his way back to his native Scotland, signing for Motherwell, managed by one of his all-time heroes, Jock Wallace. It was on his debut for them that he set up that 'family at war' goal against Rangers.

After a three-year spell at Motherwell, Ian headed for the sunny climes of Cyprus, playing with or against a number of ex-pats, such as Donnie Gillies, Peter Cormack and Kevin Mabbutt. Ironically, whereas that trio had arrived at Cyprus via Bristol, Ian made the journey the other way round, signing for Bobby Gould at Bristol Rovers in 1986.

That was to be the start of nine-and-a-half years with Rovers, although it was the arrival of Gerry Francis as manager that saw him switch from winger to full-back. 'Yes, it was Gerry who saw something that told him I'd do better at the back, and as long as I was in the side, I was happy,' said Ian.

Ian went on to complete over 400 games for The Pirates, and vividly remembers their FA Cup match at Anfield. 'An absolutely amazing atmosphere – the noise was deafening and our supporters were magnificent. I played the first half marking Steve McMahon and then, in the second half, they brought on Ian Rush for me to face!' Rovers were to go down 2-1, but gave the mighty Liverpool a real fright:

> We gave it our best shot and certainly didn't disgrace ourselves. We actually took the lead through Carl Saunders and they only got the winner ten minutes from time. There were also the play-off matches, Wembley, derbies against City – so many wonderful memories.

But, like all footballers, the day dawns when it's time to call it a day. Since leaving professional soccer, Ian has built himself a career in the construction industry, although he still enjoys his sport. For nearly three years he helped former teammate Phil Purnell manage Yate Town and he also enjoys a round of golf.

Ian Alexander in action for Bristol Rovers.

Ian Alexander today.

LEE ARCHER

The first Rovers player to score a League goal at The Memorial Stadium was left-winger Lee Archer, who also made the record books by being one of the last 'Gasheads' to score at Millwall's old ground, The Den.

'I remember both goals very well,' said Lee, who runs the Pro-Fitness Gym in Clifton. 'The goal at Millwall was my first for Rovers, and everyone remembers their first goal. It was a twenty-five yarder, but was not particularly relevant, as we were already relegated, although we did win 3-1.' And that goal at The Mem? 'A header against Stockport County that went in off the bar,' he recalled with a smile.

Born in Bristol in 1972, Lee started on schoolboy forms with Rovers aged eleven. After progressing through the Youth Training Scheme, he was signed up as a full professional by Gerry Francis, just after his eighteenth birthday.

'It was Martin Dobson who gave me my debut, and they don't get much tougher than a local derby with City at Ashton Gate,' said Lee. After just a handful of appearances in his first two seasons as a pro, Lee staked his place in the first team in the 1993/94 season, virtually an ever-present with 37 starts and five goals:

> I played under Gerry Francis, Martin Dobson, Dennis Rofe, Malcolm Allison, John Ward and Ian (Ollie) Holloway during my time at Rovers. John Ward and his assistant Dennis Booth were the best I played under. They created a fantastic team spirit at the club.

But, after 126 (plus 25 sub) League appearances and 19 goals, persistent problems with knee injuries forced Lee to leave full-time football in 1997 and he signed for then part-time non-Leaguers Yeovil Town:

> That went OK and my knee settled down, so much so that, after 30 games for The Glovers, I was persuaded to go back into full-time soccer with Rushden and Diamonds, just before they got into the Football League. Looking back, that was a mistake, as the old knee problems resurfaced under the strain of full-time soccer and I had to call it a day.

Looking to the longer-term future, Lee had already got involved in 'the fitness business' as more and more people became health conscious and wanted to attain a good level of fitness. 'I never had any intention to become a football manager or coach, and I'd spent so much time working out in the gym to recuperate from injuries and operations, it seemed a good ideal to go into that line of work,' he revealed.

For the past five years Lee has successfully worked in the fitness business. 'We specialise in one-to-one training and work on appointments only,' said Lee during a breather from one training session. 'We get all sorts of people – business men and women, golfers, housewives, office staff and so on.'

Married to Emma, the couple live at Wraxall, near Bristol. Lee has a baby daughter Ava and teenage stepdaughter Tallulah.

Left: Lee in action for Rovers.

Below: Lee gives one-to-one fitness training to a client.

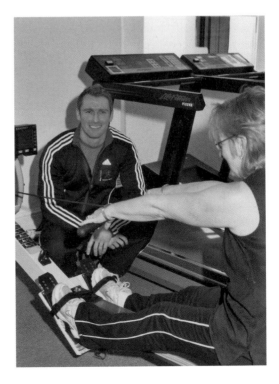

VIC BARNEY

Former Rovers man Vic Barney joins a fairly exclusive band of ex-Bristol footballers who have followed their dads into the local professional soccer scene. Of course there are the Mabbutts, and over at (dare I print the word) City, Don and Brian Clark, to give just two examples. Back in the late 1940s, a certain Vic Barney had a spell with City. In later years, his son (also called Vic) turned out in Rovers colours. 'I was actually meant to follow dad's footsteps and sign for City, but they had so many players on their books that I set off for Eastville and ended up signing for Rovers,' said Vic, a wing half or inside forward, who had six seasons with The Pirates back in the sixties.

Vic's decision to try his luck at Eastville was sound, as the club had embarked on a very successful youth policy. 'There were some very good young players there at the same time as me, including Ray Graydon, Larry Lloyd and Stuart Taylor. It was an excellent youth set-up,' he pointed out.

These days football apprentices are perhaps a little bit pampered, compared to the old days. They don't sweep terraces or clean players' boots anymore. 'When I joined the club one of my heroes was Ian Hamilton... so I was quite happy to find I'd be the one who had to look after his boots,' said Vic.

After a handful of first-team games, Vic's best season came in 1968/69, when Fred Ford promoted a lot of young players. 'Fred was a very good manager who was very loyal to his players,' pointed out Vic. 'We were a good young side and had a good cup run that year.'

Having played a couple of dozen games and scored three times that season, Vic could have been forgiven for thinking his future with Rovers was bright. But the following year he rarely featured, and Rovers let him go. 'Obviously a disappointment, but you have to get on with life,' summed up Vic.

After Rovers, Vic got a job with Rolls Royce, working in their commercial department, while still playing football for non-League Glastonbury. 'The manager was ex-Rovers winger George Petherbridge. In fact, it was a bit like a Rovers old boys club, with Ronnie Briggs and Dave Stone among the ex-Pirates there,' said Vic.

After three seasons at Glastonbury, Vic moved on to Trowbridge, which was managed by another former Rovers man, Johnny Petts. He completed the hat-trick of playing for managers who used to play at Eastville by going on to (the late) Doug Hillard's Mangotsfield.

Away from the soccer field Vic spent thirty years with Rolls Royce. After that he tried his hand at being a postman but, as he says, 'after years of football the knees and hips just weren't up to it.' These days he works as a part-time delivery driver for a pharmacy in Staple Hill and also acts as an out-of-hours driver for doctors who need to be rushed to emergency night cases.

Married to Julia, the couple live in Staple Hill.

Right: Vic in his Rovers days.

Below: Vic today, ready to answer the call.

PHIL BATER

Everything's 'coming up roses' for Phil Bater. For three years after walking away from the manager's job at his beloved Bristol Rovers, Phil successfully guided Clevedon Town to the Southern League Division One West championship. And, when he's not at The Hand Stadium, he's probably looking after those roses in his role as a landscape gardener:

> It's been great to be back. I had eighteen months out of the game after what happened at Rovers. It knocked me for six, but I'm not bitter. Life is all about learning from situations and I certainly learnt from what happened.

Phil had answered an SOS from the club he played over 350 games for, stepping into the manager's seat when the club was going through turmoil. Despite his 100 per cent commitment to the club – something that all true Rovers fans recognised and appreciated - his departure could have been handled better.

A tough-tackling defender, Phil joined Rovers as an apprentice in 1973. After impressing in the reserves, Phil made his debut against Aston Villa. Ironically he was marking former Rovers star Ray Graydon, a very good goalscoring winger and the man he replaced as Rovers manager. Phil came out on top.

By the end of the 1980/81 season, Phil had notched up over 200 League appearances for The Pirates and appeared for the Welsh Under-21 side. After relegation in 1981, Rovers, always a selling club out of financial necessity, accepted a £50,000 offer from Wrexham and Phil was on his way to North Wales. After 73 League matches for them, Phil came back to Rovers for a knockdown £5,000.

On his return, Phil was employed mainly in midfield, clocking up nearly 100 more senior appearances, during which time Rovers were certainly a force to be reckoned with in the old Third Division. Another move, this time to Brentford, saw him play 19 times for The Bees, before he took the opportunity to sign for his home-town club of Cardiff.

What should have been a dream move turned sour in his very first game for The Bluebirds: 'We were playing my old club Wrexham, we lost three-nil and I got sent off – I think I'm in their record books as the only player to get sent off making his debut for them!' Despite this, Phil notched up 76 League appearances for the club, before calling it a day on his time as a professional footballer and concentrating on his landscape gardening business:

> My dad was a gardener and when I was at Rovers the first time around, I was conscious of the need to have something to turn to when I finished playing. So I started up the gardening business and would often drive away from training with the car loaded up with gardening equipment to go on to a landscaping job.

Home for Phil and his partner Jane is in Hanham, Bristol. Phil has two sons – Sam, who works for his dad, and Geraint – from his previous marriage, while Jane has a son and a daughter.

Left: Phil in his Rovers days.

Below: Flower power is the order of the day for landscape gardener Phil today.

PETER BEADLE

'Watch out – Beadle's about!' Opposing defenders would have done well to heed that warning when Peter Beadle, wearing Rovers' blue and white quarters, was on the rampage. And, with a return of 42 goals from 112 starts, he became a Rovers favourite.

Peter, an old fashioned centre forward, started his League career at Gillingham. His wholehearted displays soon caught the eyes of the scouts from the higher divisions and a dream move materialised when Terry Venables signed him for Spurs. Unfortunately, Venables was soon replaced by Ossie Ardilles and it was time for Peter to pack his bags. 'I guess one of them liked me and the other didn't!' he said philosophically.

Following loan spells at Bournemouth and Southend, Peter moved to Elton John's Watford, where he enjoyed moderate success, making 23 appearances. But it was his next move – to Rovers – where he really came into his own. The TV catchphrase 'Beadle's About' became a favourite of the Rovers fans, as Peter enjoyed the best spell of his career, with a goal average of better than one every three games.

His first ever hat-trick – against Bury – and hitting the net on three occasions for Rovers at Ashton Gate went a long way to ingratiating himself with the Rovers faithful.

After three years at Rovers, Peter moved on to Port Vale (23 games) and then Notts County (22 games) before returning to Bristol to sign for 'the old enemy' – City. Never an easy task, moving from one side of the city to the other, but Peter enjoyed moderate success at Ashton Gate, netting 14 goals from 82 games, before hitting the trail again at the end of the 2001/02 season.

Peter tried his luck at Brentford, but his short time there was a disaster. He got sent off on his debut, was then out of action due to injury and was released. He moved on to Barnet and then joined former teammate Brian Parkin at Team Bath.

Peter joined the Clevedon Town revolution after that, taking up the post of commercial manager. But, with one eye on becoming a football manager, he took up the challenge of managing Southern League side Taunton Town. The challenge of managing a full-time club came next and Peter moved on to take the managerial reins at Conference side Newport County. 'I've worked under a lot of managers in my career – some good and some not so good,' said Peter. 'I feel I've learnt something from all of them and want to put some of the better things I've learnt into practice.'

Above: On the ball for Rovers.

Right: Peter photographed during his time with Taunton.

WELCOME TO THE TAUNTON TOWN FOOTBALL CLUB

FRANKIE BENNETT

As a more than useful winger, making accurate deliveries was food and drink for Frankie Bennett. So, when his playing days were over, he went to work for one of the leading delivery services in the country. 'I've been with the firm about four years now,' said the former Rovers man. 'It's a lot different from life as a footballer, but I enjoy it.'

Birmingham-born Frankie first kicked a football in earnest when he signed for non-League Halesowen Town in August 1992. His dazzling wing play soon had the scouts arriving at the West Midlands club to check him out and within six months he was signed by Southampton. He made his debut for Saints at Blackburn Rovers, and in his second appearance for the club scored in a 3-1 win against Chelsea at Stamford Bridge. 'That was interesting because former Prime Minister John Major, who is a big Chelsea supporter, was in the stands,' said Frankie.

In October 1996, after a handful of games for Southampton, Frankie was loaned out to Shrewsbury Town:

> That worked out quite well, as my last game for them was against the Rovers. I must have done OK, because shortly after, Ollie (Rovers manager Ian Holloway) came in for me. What struck me was that he obviously cared passionately about the club and that was a big influence in me signing for them.

When he was fit and on form, Frankie was outstanding, once scoring a twenty-five yarder against Notts County and winning the Man of the Match award. In the spring of 1997, Frankie had an operation on his troublesome knee and was out of first-team action for around a year. When he did come back, he scored a rare header in a 4-3 win at Macclesfield and followed that up with a goal in the first leg of the play-off semi-finals against Northampton:

> We took a 3-1 lead to Northampton and were favourites to get through to the play-off final. But it all went wrong. We just didn't perform, lost three-nil and missed out. It was one of the lowest points of my career.

With injuries still restricting his appearances for Rovers – around fifty in total (including as substitute) – the club let him go early in 2000. He had a short spell at Exeter City, before dropping into non-League football with Forest Green. During his time there he was a half-time substitute in the FA Vase final against Canvey Island. He went on to play for Cinderford, Aberystwyth, Weston-super-Mare and Bath City, before winding down his playing days with Brislington.

Having settled in the Bristol area, Frankie lives in Hanham with his wife Michelle and young daughters, Shane'e and Josh.

Left: Frankie in his Rovers days.

Below: Delivery driving is all part and parcel of Frankie's life today.

ALFIE BIGGS

You couldn't possibly think of writing a book about Bristol Rovers without including the man who is 'Mister Bristol Rovers' – the one and only Alfie Biggs. 'This club means so much to me,' said Alfie. 'They took up the biggest part of my footballing career and I love the club dearly.'

Ironically, Alfie, who originally lived in the 'red half of the city' – Knowle West – nearly became a Bristol City player, but was rejected by The Robins as a teenager. So he made the journey five or six miles down the road to Eastville, where he became a Rovers legend, earning the nickname 'The Baron' from his teammates for his snazzy dress sense. 'Rovers really were a local club in the true sense of the word,' said Alfie. 'When I got into the team in 1953, nine of the side were Bristolians.'

During Alfie's first seven seasons at the club, Rovers never finished lower than seventh in the Second Division, narrowly missed out on promotion to the top flight by just four points, and defeated 'The Busby Babes' of Manchester United (two years before the Munich Air Disaster) by four goals to nil, with Alfie getting two of the goals. 'Yes, that was certainly one of the major highlights in my career,' agreed Alfie.

But, despite his love of Rovers, Alfie packed his bags in 1961 to replace Tom Finney at Preston North End. Jimmy Milne, Preston's manager, described Alfie as the best player he had ever bought and Alfie's 22 goals in 49 appearances add testimony to that comment. But Alfie still hankered for Eastville's greyhound track, flower beds, and the smell of the gas manufacturing works, and he delighted Rovers fans young and old by returning home eighteen months later.

One of Alfie's biggest disappointments was seeing his beloved Rovers drop down into what was then the Third Division. But this just meant that there were Third Division defenders to torment instead of Second Division defenders, as Alfie went on to notch up 463 games for Rovers and was only three short of a double century of goals.

But, coming into the twilight of his footballing days in the 1967/68 season, Alfie found himself bidding farewell to Rovers for a second time, with Walsall snapping up Rovers' favourite son in a shock transfer. And therein lies a strange story, as local soccer folklore has it that Alfie only agreed to the transfer on condition that he could have a Rovers season ticket for life. Fact or fiction? 'Absolutely true,' replied Alfie.

After a couple of dozen games and nine goals for the Midlands club, Alfie had one last move – joining Swansea in 1968/69, where he completed his career with 16 appearances and four goals.

After soccer, Alfie finished his working life as a member of the security team at Bristol University, before he retired and moved to Poole with his wife Marion. The couple have two daughters and a son, plus five grandchildren.

Right: Alfie in his Rovers days.

Below: Time to reflect for one of Rovers' all-time greats.

BOB BLOOMER

With Rovers' promotion drive gathering increased momentum, manager Gerry Francis decided he needed to strengthen his squad. He remembered the young Chesterfield full-back who always seemed to stand out in his games against Rovers and so it was, on transfer deadline day that March, Bob Bloomer came to join Rovers. 'Gerry told me that he always kept tabs on players that consistently played well against his teams and that he wanted me in the squad for that final big push,' said Bob.

Bob began his soccer journey as a schoolboy on Sheffield Wednesday's books. Turned down for a professional contract, he played local non-League football while pursuing a career as a plasterer, working for a local company which specialised in ornate wall borders and decorative fire surrounds. But he hadn't given up his dream of becoming a professional footballer and wrote off to a number of League clubs in the hope of getting a second chance. Countless letters later he was invited to Chesterfield, where he came through a successful trial period to sign on for the club.

'John Duncan, the former Spurs forward, was the manager there at the time and I shall always be grateful to him for giving me that second chance,' said Bob. Over the next five seasons he made 127 (plus 24 sub) appearances for The Spireites, including five games against Rovers. A versatile player, he played at full-back, midfield and even upfront for the side, scoring 15 goals for the club before his move to Bristol:

> The boss saw me primarily as a right-back, but Ian 'Jocky' Alexander was the man keeping me out. Gerry showed a lot of faith in his players and if you did well you stayed in the side, which was fair enough. I remember playing against City at Ashton Gate and their winger, Alan Walsh, gave me a right roasting. We lost four-nil, but I got my own back in the return fixture when we won one-nil and I got the goal.

In 1992, after 22 games (including sub appearances) for Rovers, Bob departed to begin an adventure with Cheltenham Town, which continues to this day. 'Cheltenham were still very much a non-League side in those days – The Beezer Homes League I think – but, under the management of Steve Cottrell, were on a roller coaster ride of success,' he said proudly. An FA Trophy win at Wembley was surpassed by promotion in 1996 to the 'promised land' – the Football League – with Bob playing his part with nearly 100 appearances and eight goals.

After hanging up his boots, Bob has been assistant manager and caretaker manager at Whaddon Road. These days he's in charge of the youth team, helping to bring on the young talent that could be first-team stars of the future.

Bob and his wife Cath live in Bradley Stoke with their two children – thirteen-year-old daughter Megan, who is a tidy player in women's soccer, and ten-year-old Alex who prefers music to football.

Above: Bob Bloomer on the ball, playing against Rovers.

Right: Off to work.

RONNIE BRIGGS

'Make sure you get the name right,' said the former Bristol Rovers goalkeeper. 'There's an R in Briggs – I don't want the boys in blue coming round to talk to me about the Great Train Robbery!' Still, if your name happens to be Ronnie Briggs ('don't forget the R') you've every right to want it spelt correctly, especially as our man works as a security guard.

Originally from Belfast, the likeable Irishman began his career at Manchester United no less. 'I was spotted by a United scout when I was playing schoolboy football,' explained Ronnie. A brave and talented goalkeeper, Ronnie's skills between the posts blossomed under the expert coaching that has always been part of the Old Trafford success story. 'The trouble was that I was one of seven goalkeepers on the books. Harry Gregg was the number one keeper at that time, so it was always going to be hard to get into the first team.'

Ronnie eventually broke into United's firsts and enjoyed a run in the team, managed, of course, by Sir Matt Busby. 'An awesome figure, who commanded respect,' was Ronnie's summing-up of Sir Matt.

With three schoolboy caps and an Under-21 cap to his name, Ronnie's displays earned him a call-up to the full Northern Ireland team, playing in the preliminary rounds of the World Cup… 'and then some bloke called Pat Jennings turned up, and that was that!'

Looking for regular first-team football, Ronnie moved on to Swansea, then playing in the old Second Division. 'The manager there was a man called Trevor Morris. He got sacked the same season, though I don't think it was all my fault!' laughed Ronnie.

In 1966 Ronnie was on his travels, this time to join Bristol Rovers at Eastville. At that time he was one of three goalkeepers competing for the no.1 shirt. In pole position was local lad Bernard Hall, but a bad head injury brought an end to Bernard's career and Ronnie got his chance to claim the position.

Sadly for Ronnie, his own career was brought to a premature end when he took a hefty kick in the hands as he went to collect the ball – and he still bears the scars today. 'Ironically it was one of my own teammates who was trying to clear the ball and caught me instead,' he revealed.

Ronnie dropped out of League Football and into the Western League, playing for Frome Town and Glastonbury. But his hands were getting no better and he called it a day. Having been a custodian of his goal for so long, Ronnie plumped for a career as a general custodian – working as a security guard. 'I had eighteen years with Brinks – but that gold bullion robbery was nothing to do with me!' he joked. For the past seven years he has been with Reliance Security.

Ronnie and his wife Ena live in Frenchay. They have three children and seven grandchildren.

Left: Goalkeeper Ronnie Briggs in action.

Below: Making sure everything's secure.

SIMON BRYANT

It was a proud moment for Simon Bryant when he was handed the captain's armband and told he would be leading out the side. He was Rovers' youngest captain at just seventeen years of age. 'I'd been involved with Rovers since I was eight years old, so to be given the chance to captain the side at seventeen was definitely an honour for me,' said Simon.

A product of Rovers' youth policy, Simon has nothing but praise for the coaches at the club. 'Roy Dolling was exceptional, also Tony Gill and Phil Bater, who was a large part of my life and someone I still keep in touch with,' he said.

In addition to going on to captain Rovers, Simon is also the third youngest player in the club's history to play in a League match for the first team. Aged just sixteen when he made his debut, only Ronnie Dix and Scott Sinclair were younger debutants.

He also has another record, one that he didn't particularly want — he was the first Rovers substitute to be sent off!

Looking back on his time with Rovers, Simon praises former teammate Andy Tillson. 'Andy's been there and done it, so he looked after me when I got in the side and took me under his wing,' he said. 'Also, we had Jason Roberts — what a player. I always knew he'd make it to the top.'

Not that goalscoring was one of Simon's specialities. After 65 starts and 22 substitute appearances, he'd got the grand total of two goals! 'That's right,' laughed Simon. 'Cambridge away and Rochdale at home — so you could say I was a consistent goalscorer home and away!' In fairness, like older brother Matt who played for arch rivals City, he spent practically all of his career in defence.

But, despite Simon's dedication and long association with Rovers, he was released by the club in 2003. 'It was a real body blow at the time. I'd been with the club for as long as I could remember and at twenty-one I was finished there.'

After Rovers Simon went to Conference side Forest Green, but after just a handful of games injured himself in training and had to have surgery on his right knee. 'I tried to make a comeback with Team Bath, but the knee wasn't up to it so that was that,' he revealed.

A single man, Simon lives with his parents in Hanham. He can often be found at Bath University, where he is taking a two-year course to be a coach. 'My long-term aim is to be a professional soccer coach or even manager one day,' he confided. And, as one of the youngest players to don Rovers' blue and white quarters, and the club's youngest ever captain, who would bet against Simon becoming Rovers' youngest ever manager one day.

Left: Simon in action for Rovers.

Below: Taking a break from his coaching course, Simon Bryant today.

BOBBY CAMPBELL

Bristol Rovers certainly got their money's worth with Bobby Campbell. Not that he ever played for them. In fact, that's probably the only job he hasn't filled for the club, having been manager, physiotherapist, coach and trainer, to name a few of his roles with The Pirates.

Born in Glasgow in 1922, Bobby's first real involvement in football came when he was a ball boy at his local Scottish club, Partick Thistle. After playing for junior club Glasgow Perthshire, Bobby was offered terms with Falkirk. The start of the Second World War put that on hold, and during his time in the army he played for the Army & Armed Services representative side overseas.

At the end of hostilities Bobby signed for Hibernian, moving south in 1947 when Chelsea shelled out £12,000 (a tidy sum in those days) to bring him to England. 'My first game was against Aston Villa and there was over 60,000 in the crowd at Stamford Bridge,' said Bobby.

Bobby's form soon came to the attention of the Scotland selectors and he went on to win five caps. 'The highlight of my playing days was being picked to play for Scotland against Switzerland at Hampden Park, before a crowd of nearly 124,000' said Bobby.

After nearly 200 games and 38 goals for Chelsea, Bobby moved to Reading where he played for the best part of three years, before at the age of thirty-five, he moved into coaching. Leaving Reading in 1961, Bobby took the post of manager at Dumbarton, but after a year in charge of the Scottish part-timers, he left to start his love affair with Bristol Rovers. 'I started as trainer and coach, but over the years there weren't many jobs that I didn't do – you name it, I did it,' he said proudly.

The loyal and dedicated Bobby Campbell played a vital part in the spotting, developing, and coaching of future stars like Paul Randall, Steve White and Gary Mabbutt. In 1977, with the club facing relegation, Bobby took over the manager's hot seat and, assisted by coaches Harold Jarman and Bobby Gould, saved the club from dropping down to the Third Division, as well as taking them on a giant-killing cup run.

During his time in charge he gave the likes of Gary Mabbutt, Steve White, Paul Randall and Welsh goalkeeper Martin Thomas their chance to make names for themselves – they all went on to be big money transfers to higher league clubs. And forget the old saying that Scots are tight with money – he was Rovers' first manager to spend £100,000 on a player – Stewart Barrowclough from Birmingham City.

In December 1979 Bobby stepped down from the high-pressure job of managing Rovers but continued to coach young players. These days, now in his eighties, he lives in Almondsbury with his partner Esther, and despite a recent knee replacement operation, still gets out and about on the golf course. But when it comes to sport, soccer in the form of Bristol Rovers, is his number one choice.

Above: Bobby Campbell (far right) in a 1960s Rovers photocall.

Right: Bobby today, with one of the Scotland shirts he wore.

BILLY CLARK

Over the course of their careers many footballers pick up nicknames. When Billy Clark joined Bristol Rovers in 1987, he wasn't to know that he would spend so much time on the bench (he actually set a Rovers club record of being named substitute 64 times) that he would become known as 'The Judge'!

Primarily a central defender, Billy's progress at Rovers was halted by a succession of injuries, plus the form of central defenders Steve Yates and Geoff Twentyman. Originally from Christchurch in Hampshire, Billy had four years at his local Football League club Bournemouth. 'I joined Rovers in 1987, initially on three months' loan,' said Billy. 'It went well and Rovers paid a £12,000 fee to take me on permanently.'

Billy was to enjoy a ten-year spell at Rovers, and despite lengthy spells on the bench or in the treatment room, went on to play over 300 games for The Pirates.

'There were some good times at Rovers – playing against Liverpool at Anfield, getting to Wembley, promotion – lots of good memories,' he recalled. And what about managers? 'Yes, they had quite a few while I was there – Gerry Francis, Dennis Rofe, Martin Dobson, Steve Cross, Malcolm Allison, John Ward. John was probably the best, while Malcolm Allison was an interesting guy,' he said.

In 1997 it was time for Billy to say farewell to Rovers, although it says much for his popularity that over 8,000 people turned up for his testimonial against a West Ham side that included Rio Ferdinand, Frank Lampard, Ian Wright and John Hartson. Billy moved 'down the road' to Exeter City in Division Three, playing over fifty games for The Grecians.

After eighteen months at Exeter, Billy went to Forest Green Rovers, where his two-year spell included playing for them at Aston Villa in the final of the FA Trophy. He had a further two years at Newport County, before moving on to Weston-super-Mare in the Nationwide Conference (South). A qualified coach, Billy held the position of youth development officer there, as well as coaching at Weston College.

He moved on to Clevedon Town, where he played a starring role in the side winning the Southern League Division One West championship and also their headline-grabbing FA Cup run.

Married to Bristol girl Nickki, the couple live at Warmley and have a young son, Bailey.

And, one last question for Billy. Going back through his career, who was the toughest centre forward he's had to mark? 'Dion Dublin, without a doubt,' is his instant reply. And he should know – after all, he's not a bad 'judge'!

Left: Billy (right) challenges for the ball during his Rovers days.

Below: Billy Clark enjoys his football at Clevedon these days.

JOE DAVIS

It seems a little ironic that Joe Davis, whose sterling performances between 1960 and 1967 in the heart of the Bristol Rovers defence often got him headlines in the local press, turned to newspapers when he gave up playing. First he ran a newsagents shop for about eighteen months and then he joined the staff of the local evening paper, where he worked for thirty years, before retiring as field sales manager.

Joe was spotted by a Rovers scout playing for Soundwell's local youth team and was signed up by The Pirates in 1957. Joe's cousin Bobby Jones was in the same youth side and he too joined Rovers, playing alongside Joe over the years.

A thinking footballer rather than a stopper, Joe played most of his 230-plus senior games at centre half and commanded the respect of teammates and opposition alike. For many years he skippered the Rovers team, and although not the tallest centre half in the world, he was rarely beaten in the air. He was also deceptively fast, sure in the tackle, and could quickly break up an opposing attack and set up a counter-attack before the opposition could regroup:

> There was a wonderful team spirit about Rovers and some great characters in the team. There was also something very special about the old ground at Eastville, with its smell of gas wafting over from the Gas Board's manufacturing plant next door, the flower beds behind the goals and the dog racing track around the pitch – yes, I don't think there was another ground like it in the country – unique.

Towards the end of his time with Rovers, Joe dropped back to the full-back position, but, as is a footballer's lot, there usually comes a parting of the ways, no matter how much you love a club. Joe moved on to spend eighteen months with Swansea, notching up 38 appearances for the Welsh club, before injury in the form of an Achilles problem brought an end to his playing days. But it wasn't all bad news for Joe. He went back to his beloved Bristol Rovers, helping them as a scout and youth development coach. And he's proud of the fact that many of the youngsters he worked with – players like Gary Penrice, Ian Holloway, Phil Purnell, Paul Randall and Steve White – went on to become stars at Bristol Rovers.

On the domestic front, Joe has been married for over forty-six years to wife Alma. They live in the Kingswood area and have three daughters and four grandchildren.

Opposite above: Joe Davis (centre, with head bandaged) plays through the pain barrier for Rovers.

Opposite below: Time to reflect on his long and illustrious career at Bristol Rovers.

GRAHAM DAY

He's played with and against some of the best players in the world. Pele, Cruyff, Gerd Muller, George Best, Bobby Moore, Franz Beckenbauer and Carlos Alberto, to name but a few. Not bad for local lad Graham Day, who spent five years at the heart of the Bristol Rovers defence. In fairness, Graham came into contact with most of these famous names after he left Rovers in 1978 to join the soccer exodus to the American Soccer League, but more of that later.

A solid, no-nonsense centre half, Graham signed for Rovers in 1973. They had a pretty useful side in those days and home was Eastville Stadium – this was a few years before the team's exile to Bath City's 'Trumpton Park' and latterly The Memorial Stadium.

Graham went on to notch up 150 games for The Pirates. Asked about goals, he reckons he's been credited with around seven. 'Unfortunately,' he says with a smile, 'half a dozen of those were for the opposition – own goals!' So does he remember the one goal he scored FOR the Rovers? 'Oh yes. We were playing Fulham. Those were the days when they were quite an attraction in the old Second Division, having Moore, Bestie and Rodney Marsh in their team. I went up for a corner and headed it into the top corner. I say headed it, I actually caught it all wrong and it flew in off my ear – it didn't half hurt!'

In 1978 Graham got an offer he simply couldn't refuse. It was the chance to play in the newly formed American Soccer League, where many of the biggest names in the world of soccer were playing out their illustrious careers and enjoying the experience of being part of the birth of pro soccer in the States. 'I had seven years over there, playing for Portland Timbers,' he explains. 'The team was managed by my former boss at Rovers, Don Megson. It was a fantastic experience – unbelievable.'

At the end of his American adventure, Graham returned home to continue plying his trade. Having dropped down to non-League football with Forest Green and Bath City, he could have been forgiven for thinking his League playing days were over. They weren't:

> I got a call to say Bournemouth wanted to sign me, so I went. It was the same day that they also signed George Best and the home crowd's attendance jumped from 3,000 to over 8,000. I'd like to think it was because of signing me, but Bestie may have added a couple of hundred to the gate!

After four months at Bournemouth, Graham headed back to Bath City, where his playing days came to an end after he broke a leg. He went on to become a financial advisor before embarking on a complete career change and going into the licensed trade.

These days Graham, who has two sons Ryan and Matthew, runs The Flower Pot Inn at Kingswood.

Left: Centre half Graham Day during his playing days at Rovers.

Below: 'Mein Host' Graham Day.

TONY FORD

It was Liverpool's legendary Bill Shankly who once said that football wasn't a matter of life or death – it was more important than that! Well don't mention that to Tony Ford, he nearly died after suffering an injury on the soccer field.

'I was playing for Rovers at Preston and took a kick in the stomach,' explained Tony. 'I was in a bit of pain but managed to play on, but after the game I was in agony and ended up in Wigan Hospital.' Tony was to spend four or five days at the hospital, before coming home to convalesce. But the pains returned with a vengeance, and he was rushed by ambulance first to Cosham Hospital, and then to Frenchay. 'It turned out to be a ruptured spleen and I was very ill,' said Tony. 'In fact, my wife Margaret was told to prepare for the worse.'

Happily, Tony pulled through, although the injury did spell the end of his playing days, after 'a season and a bit' at Rovers, at the age of just twenty-five.

It was with Bristol City that Tony had made his mark. Between 1961 and 1968 Tony made 186 senior appearances for the Robins, scoring 12 goals – all penalties – in the process.

In 1968 Tony lost his place in the side and was transferred down the road to Rovers. 'Once you've been a first-team regular, reserve-team football is not for you, so when Rovers came in for me I jumped at it,' said Tony.

But if Alan Dicks didn't rate Tony, Rovers manager Bill Dodgin did. After signing the tall right-back, Dodgin appointed him team captain – and penalty taker. It was all going well – too well – for Tony. After 25 games (and a successful penalty) things were looking good. And then, as we all know, life has a way of kicking you in the guts – in Tony's case, quite literally. 'And that was that,' he summed up.

After hanging up his boots, Tony had a spell on the coaching staff at Plymouth Argyle. Later he became assistant manager at Hereford United, winning the Third Division championship, before moving north to become assistant to Bobby Moncur at Hearts. 'When Bobby left I was appointed manager,' said Tony. 'I thought, given the club's lack of cash and the fact that Rangers and Celtic were dominating the Scottish League, we were doing OK. After all, we were third in the league.' But the chairman decided on change and Tony was on his way.

'After that I left football altogether and went for a "proper job" with a bit more security,' said Tony with a smile. He worked for ten years as a sales rep with Marley Tiles – then got made redundant. Undeterred with life in 'Civvy Street', Tony became a rep for a company making road surface materials. This lasted another five years, before Tony was made redundant again. 'So much for job security!' These days Tony is a driving instructor – obviously still very much a 'pass master!'

Tony and Margaret live in Thornbury. They have three children – twins Daren and Louise, and eldest son Mike who followed in dad's footsteps, having played for Cardiff and Oxford. They are also the proud grandparents of eight grandchildren.

Above: Tony Ford clears the ball under pressure.

Right: In the driving seat, instructor Tony Ford.

GERRY FRANCIS

Soccer legend Gerry Francis first came to Bristol Rovers in 1987, taking up the role of player/manager. Within three years he had guided the club to the (old) Third Division championship and also to the final of the Freight Rover Trophy at Wembley, with Rovers going down 2-1 to Tranmere:

> We were called 'Rag Bag Rovers' when I arrived in 1987. No ground of our own, we had no money, trained at a chocolate factory and had to change in Portakabins, I even lent the club £10,000 so that we could sign Ian Holloway – not that I'd advise other managers to do this!

Prior to Rovers, Gerry's first managerial appointment was at Exeter City in 1983. Despite his vast experience in the game, plus his presence as a player on the pitch, he was unable to stop the troubled club sliding into the Fourth Division and Gerry and the club parted company.

> I had only ever played and coached the highest level. I thought I knew most things and could handle management easily. Then I went to Exeter. I learnt that management is a totally different game and that it doesn't matter what you did as a player or a coach, when you manage you learn a whole new trade. I made a load of mistakes with a bunch of honest players who, technically, couldn't do what I wanted them to. But I learnt so much.

Prior to stepping into the managerial cauldron, Gerry had made quite a name for himself as one of soccer's finest midfield players. After nearly 300 games, many as captain, for his first club Queens Park Rangers, he moved to Crystal Palace for around half-a-million pounds. By that time he had made a dozen appearances for England, with Don Revie appointing him captain: When he skippered England at twenty-three he was the youngest captain of the national side since Bobby Moore.

> Obviously, playing for England is a proud and fantastic feeling for any player, but going on to captain England, especially at such a young age, is something special and can never be taken away from you.

A return to Loftus Road followed in 1981, before Gerry moved on to wear the colours of Coventry City, Swansea, Cardiff and Portsmouth, before managing Exeter and then Rovers.

His success, achieved on a shoestring budget at Rovers, saw him return to QPR as manager. He followed that with three years as manager of Spurs, before returning to the QPR hot seat. In 2001, he returned to Rovers. 'I had retired at QPR, but with Rovers relegated to Division Three, as it was then, I agreed to come back for a year,' said Gerry. 'Unfortunately, I only managed the club for about twenty games; due to having two very close members of my family being in intensive care, I resigned at Christmas.' Sadly, both Gerry's relatives passed away.

Away from football, Gerry lives in Bagshot, Surrey with his wife Julie and three young children, Adam, Chloe and Jake. A lifelong pigeon enthusiast, he raised a few eyebrows when he got involved in promoting and investing in the musical, *125th Street*.

Since leaving Rovers, Gerry has resisted numerous approaches to return to soccer. He has a weekly programme on Sky Sports and does a lot of media work for TV and radio.

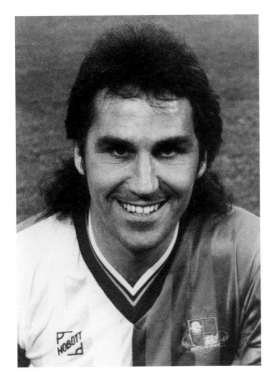

Left: Gerry during his Rovers days.

Below: A toast, in orange squash, to the future success of Rovers.

BOBBY GOULD

The man who's played with more clubs than Tiger Woods, that's Bobby Gould. And among those many clubs are both Bristol sides, with Bobby also having two spells managing the Rovers.

Bobby, a goalscoring centre forward, started his career with his local club Coventry City. He went on to play for Arsenal, and was in the side that got beaten by Swindon Town in that famous League Cup final defeat, although he did get Arsenal's goal in a 3-1 defeat. Other clubs that benefited from his goalscoring skills included West Bromwich Albion, Wolves (twice) and West Ham United.

Bristol City manager Alan Dicks brought Gould to Ashton Gate in December 1972. During his eleven-month spell with The Robins he netted 19 goals in 43 appearances, before being transferred back to the top flight to West Ham.

After adding a lot more goals and clubs to his CV, Bobby came back to Bristol when Rovers manager Don Megson paid Wolves £10,000 for his signature. He made the best possible start, scoring a hat-trick on his debut, a Second Division match against Blackburn Rovers.

Bobby went on to play 40 senior games for Rovers, netting 13 goals in the process, but after Don Megson gave up his managerial role at Rovers, he was on his way again, this time to Hereford as player-coach. He went on to take on player-coach roles at Aldershot and then Chelsea, before he got the call to replace Terry Cooper as Rovers manager.

Ironically, he could have been Rovers shortest-serving manager ever – less than twenty-four hours – when he threatened to quit after learning that most of the senior players were on better salaries than him. Bobby made sure that was soon rectified!

During that two-year spell in charge, Bobby used his knowledge of the game to bring in a number of new players to boost the team. Two of the biggest names he signed were Allan Ball and Mick Channon, who were in the twilight of their careers.

After two years in charge, Bobby left to manage his old club Coventry. Two years later he was back. The Coventry job hadn't worked out and he was invited to succeed the departing David Williams. Again he used his network of contacts to improve Rovers' playing staff, with Gerry Francis coming in as player/coach.

It was during Bobby's second reign that a cash crisis forced Rovers out of the spiritual Eastville home and they became lodgers at Bath City's Twerton Park. 'To say the facilities weren't very good would be something of an understatement, but we just had to make the best of it,' said Bobby.

And the club was still in deep financial trouble. 'Things were so tight that one week they had to sell my club car in order to pay the wages,' he pointed out.

As is the way with football management nothing stays the same, and after another two year spell in the hot seat, Bobby's second spell at Rovers ended when he left to manage Wimbledon. It was there that he enjoyed one of his greatest soccer triumphs, leading them to victory in that famous one-nil FA Cup final win over Liverpool.

After Wimbledon, Bobby had spells as assistant manager at QPR and Peterborough, and also as manager at West Brom and Cheltenham Town. He even had a period as manager of Wales.

These days Bobby can be found at his home in Portishead with his wife Margery. They have two sons, Jonathon and Richard.

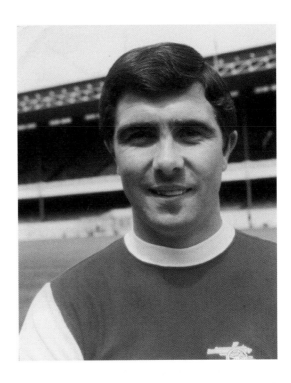

Right: Bobby during his Arsenal days.

Below: Bobby Gould today.

IAN HAMILTON

After a premature end to his football career, ex-Rovers star Ian Hamilton enjoys nothing more than sitting back and watching a good game of… cricket. In fact, he and wife Betty have travelled the globe in support of the England team:

> I've always enjoyed cricket – I used to play for Thornbury in my younger days. Betty and I are both members of Gloucestershire County Cricket Club and we've been all over the world – Australia, Barbados and South Africa in the last six years – to support the Test team.

On the football front, Ian had followed in the footsteps of his dad John, a wing half who played for Rovers before the war, and his elder brother David who was released from Rovers when he was twenty-one. Making his debut in 1958, Ian had to be content with the occasional first-team outing in the early years, as the Rovers forward line of Geoff Bradford, Dai Ward and Alfie Biggs reigned supreme. But once he had established himself in the side, he made sure his goalscoring exploits would mean a regular first-team spot and he was the club's top scorer with 22 goals at the end of the 1964/65 season. That same season he netted a hat-trick at Southend – and still finished up on the losing side, Rovers going down 6-3! The previous year it was Ian's two headed goals at Halifax that ensured The Pirates avoided the drop into the Fourth Division:

> They were a brilliant bunch of lads. I'd struck up a great partnership with Alfie (Biggs) and he did a terrific job for Rovers, not just on the pitch, but also in helping and encouraging the younger players coming through.

Ian also speaks highly of his former manager at Rovers, Bert Tann. 'I got on very well with him and I think he did an exceptional job for Bristol Rovers,' summed up Ian.

Unfortunately, a persistent knee injury which had caused him to miss a number of matches was to cut short what should have been a much longer career in League football. He had a handful of games on loan at Exeter City in the 1967/68 season and the following year he spent a season with Newport County before he called it a day, leaving professional football at the age of twenty-eight. During his time at Rovers he notched up 169 senior appearances, netting 67 goals – many of them important match-winners.

After leaving football Ian worked in the offices at Rolls Royce at Filton before taking early retirement in 1994. Like many of his fellow professionals, the wear and tear of playing professional football has taken its toll and he has undergone surgery to his knee and hip.

Living at Rudgeway, near Almondsbury where they have been for nearly thirty years, Ian and Betty have one son, a daughter and a teenage grandson.

Left: Ian Hamilton heads for goal at Eastville.

Below: Case packed and passport at the ready, Ian's never stumped for somewhere to follow cricket.

LEWIS HOGG

To call Lewis Hogg the strong silent type would probably be a bit of an understatement. A man of few words, the former tough-tackling Bristol Rovers man lets his football and his tackles do the talking for him.

Lewis joined Rovers as a youth trainee in 1999. One of the youngest players to captain The Pirates, Lewis went on to make over sixty senior appearances for the team, scoring six goals:

> During my time at Rovers I played under Ollie (Ian Holloway), Gerry Francis, Gary Thompson and, finally, Ray Graydon. I would say that Ollie was the single biggest influence on my career, a very good man manager who gets the best out of his players.

Looking back on his days in Rovers' blue and white, Lewis fondly remembers the derby games with rivals City. 'They were always a bit special, with a terrific atmosphere,' he said. Lewis also enjoyed cup ties. Of his six Rovers goals, three were in cup matches. The one that stands out is the one he got in a Football League Cup match against Everton at Goodison Park:

> They had a real star-studded side and we were given absolutely no chance of getting a result. There was a crowd of over 35,000 and I got our goal in a one-all draw. And we went on to win the replay at The Memorial Ground on penalties.

A later FA Cup tie at (then) top-flight Derby County also brings back happy memories. 'We hammered them three-one on their own ground – the first time a Division Three club had knocked out a Premiership club,' he said with a smile. 'Nathan Ellington scored a superb hat-trick and I was the captain that day, so it was a bit special.'

A member of the England Under-18 squad, Lewis was renowned for his enthusiasm and tough tackling, although this inevitably incurred the wrath of match officials on occasions, with Lewis taking an early bath in a League encounter with Reading in December 2000.

It was during the reign of Ray Graydon, with the team struggling, that Lewis was released by the club. He had an initial trial with Exeter before signing for Barnet. It was in Barnet's colours that Lewis again saw red, for a late tackle against (ironically) Exeter.

After Barnet, Lewis came back nearer home to play in the Conference South with Weston-super-Mare, before signing for Bath City last summer. A single man, Lewis lives in the Longwell Green area of Bristol. And when he's not delivering tackles and passes for The Seasiders, he's a delivery driver.

Right: Lewis in action for Rovers.

Below: Ready for another game.

IAN HOLLOWAY

If you are ever looking for the proverbial 'blue blooded male', look no further than Rovers legend and former manager Ian 'Ollie' Holloway. He's definitely got blue blood running through his veins and certainly wouldn't accept anything in red!

Ollie, as he is known to friend and foe alike, is as much a part of Bristol Rovers as the pirate motif on their shirts, having clocked up over 450 games for the club in three spells, the last as player/manager. 'I was a supporter who played for my club and I am very proud of my association with The Gas,' said Ollie.

Initially a right-winger, Ollie signed professional forms for 'his team' in 1980 and, although his heart was with Rovers, neither he nor the club could turn down the offer that took him to Wimbledon in the summer of 1985. It was never the same for Ollie with The Dons though, and a mix of injury, illness and loss of form saw him restricted to just 19 starts. A move to Brentford fared little better, where he made 30 full appearances and he even had a short spell on loan at Torquay.

A move back to Rovers in the 1987/88 season was just what the doctor ordered, with astute Rovers manager Gerry Francis actually lending the club the £10,000 that brought Ian back home. It proved to be a masterstroke, with Ollie, now playing in a tigerish midfield role, helping the club to win the Third Division championship and make the finals of the Leyland Daf Cup.

'Rovers winning the championship was one of the highest points of my career,' said Ollie proudly. There was also the little matter of beating deadly rivals City 3-0 at Twerton Park, when it looked like City would pip Rovers to the top spot. 'Icing on the cake,' he said with a smile.

Rovers without Holloway was unthinkable for Rovers fans, but in 1991 he was on the move to play in the top flight with Queens Park Rangers. During his five years there he notched up 147 appearances, before landing the job that he could only have dreamt about years before – player/manager back at Rovers. He moulded together a pretty good side, but one that kept 'just missing out' – losing out in the two-leg play-off semi-final at Northampton, despite taking a 3-1 advantage into the return match, and then falling away at the death in 2001, having led the table for so long. 'I think those two disappointments were the lowest points of my career, getting so close, but not fulfilling the dream,' said Ollie.

The failure to miss out on promotion and the play-offs in 2001 ultimately cost Ollie his job as manager at Rovers, a bitter pill to swallow for a man so committed to the cause. Gritting his teeth, he was soon back in the management saddle, returning to Queens Park Rangers. That role came to an end earlier this year, due more to boardroom politics than anything else, and he was sent on 'gardening leave'. However, you can't keep a good man down and Ollie is now the 'gaffer' at Plymouth Argyle.

Ollie is married to Kim and they have a teenage son, William, identical teenage twins Chloe and Eve and another teenage daughter, Harriet.

Left: Ollie in action for Rovers.

Below: A more recent photo of Ollie, taken when he was on 'gardening leave'!

PETER HOOPER

Which former Bristol footballer packed the hardest shot? Now there's a question guaranteed to cause debate and difference of opinion. To many the answer is easy, former Rovers and City outside left Peter Hooper.

Born in Teignmouth, Peter played representative football while serving overseas in the RAF and was also an amateur at Exeter City. 'An old school pal of mine was an amateur on Rovers books, and he recommended me to the club,' recalled Peter. 'Rovers manager Bert Tann drove out to see me and signed me without even seeing me play.'

That was in 1953 and the club had just won promotion to the old Second Division. Peter soon made the no.11 shirt his own, displacing long-serving Josser Watling who dropped back to full-back.

Back in the early days of Peter's career, most players had to take a drop in wages during the close season and so many took summer jobs to supplement their income:

I used to spend the summer as a deckchair attendant back home in Teignmouth... Somehow I can't imagine David Beckham doing that! I had nine seasons at Rovers and although I scored over 100 goals for the club (107 to be exact) I always felt that I'd never really won over Bert Tann, although his number two, Fred Ford, was always encouraging me.

Although he was to terrorise right-backs and goalkeepers alike, Peter's Rovers side was relegated in 1962. After a falling-out with Tann, Peter left to try his luck with the then Second Division club Cardiff City. 'Initially it was a good move for me, although I'd never trained so hard as I did at Cardiff,' he admitted.

After 40 games and 22 goals for the Welsh club, Peter was reunited with Fred Ford who was by then manager at Rovers' arch rivals, Bristol City. 'After being involved with Rovers for so long, it felt a bit weird putting on the red and white of City,' admitted Peter.

Between 1963 and 1966, Peter played 54 senior games for the club, scoring 14 goals, before moving into non-League football with Worcester City. After a year there he moved back to his native Devon, taking over The Three Pigeons public house in Bishops Tawton.

After ten years of pulling pints, Peter worked for the probation service and did some coaching at local schools. In between these moves, he also agreed to help out an old friend by playing for Barnstaple Town. 'I packed it in in the end, as I was playing football Saturdays and then racing back to work behind the bar,' he explained.

Ten years ago Peter was diagnosed with prostate cancer and was receiving radiotherapy treatment five days a week at Exeter Hospital for seven weeks. 'Something like that makes you see things and people in a different light,' said Peter, who has now recovered from the illness.

Peter and his wife Crystal recently celebrated their forty-eighth wedding anniversary. They have two children, Paula and Karen, and one granddaughter, Ella May.

Above: Peter (front row, far right) in his Rovers days.

Right: Back at the Rovers, Peter today.

TREVOR JACOBS

Trevor Jacobs isn't likely to ever forget his debut for Bristol Rovers in a hurry. Brighton away, with a certain Brian Clough in charge of the opposition. And Rovers absolutely hammered them:

> Because it was Brian Clough's first game in charge all the telly cameras and press were there. We'd had a mix-up with our kit, which clashed with theirs, so they lent us their away strip. We walloped them 8-2 and Cloughie was not best pleased. We could hear him ranting and raving at his side through the dressing-room wall afterwards and then he did something very 'Cloughie'. He marched into our dressing-room, collected up the kit and took it out onto the track and burnt it!

It was in 1973 that Trevor joined Rovers, having spent eight years with rivals City, who he joined as an apprentice. 'Going from City to Rovers was never ever a problem for me,' he said. 'It meant that I was getting regular first-team football and I didn't have to leave the area or move house.'

But if he has fond memories of his Rovers debut, he's got mixed feelings about his first start for City. 'It was Rotherham away and we were three down at half-time and I'd scored an own goal,' he admitted. 'On the plus side, we came back in the second half to get a draw.'

Having played 145 games in City's red and white, full-back Trevor was to enjoy 89 games over three seasons in Rovers' blue and white. 'Rovers had a fantastic striking pair in "Smash and Grab" (Alan Warboys and Bruce Bannister),' said Trevor. 'They were the main reason we did so well in the Brighton match – their defence just couldn't cope with them.'

After finishing his time at Rovers, Trevor played for Bideford in the Western League. 'I did that for a season, but, as I had gone into the pub business, I packed in playing,' he explained.

Like many former pros, the idea of running a public house appealed to Trevor. 'I had two years at The Horseshoe Inn at Shepton Mallett and then eight as landlord of The Baccy Jar at Whitchurch,' he said. 'Running a pub was very enjoyable, although the hours were a bit unsociable,' he added.

But when it comes to unsociable working hours, Trevor is obviously a glutton for punishment. After leaving the pub trade he, again like many of his former teammates, became a postman. 'I've been "on the post" now for about eighteen years,' he revealed. 'Once you've adjusted to getting up early, it's fine and the afternoons are your own.'

These days, when Trevor's finished his post round, he can be found in his home at Bedminster. Married to Mary, the couple have two sons and three grandchildren.

Left: Trevor during his playing days.

Below: Trevor today.

HAROLD JARMAN

If you were asked to select your Rovers all-time team of greats, one of the first names on the teamsheet would undoubtedly be that of Harold Jarman.

An outstanding winger, he served the Rovers as player, youth team manager (twice) and manager. During his playing days the cry 'Harold, Harold' would rise up from the Eastville terraces as he tormented opposing full-backs, turning them inside out as he flew down the flank, centring for one of his fellow strikers or cutting in to smash home one of the 143 goals he netted for The Pirates.

Harold began his long playing career for Rovers in 1959 and soon became a favourite of the Eastville faithful. An all-rounder, Harold also showed fans of Gloucester Cricket Club that he was just as useful with a cricket bat as with a football.

Harold had fourteen seasons with Rovers and was released in 1973. Determined to prove that he still had plenty to offer, he finished his League career with a season at Newport County and ended the season as the Welsh club's top scorer with 12 goals. Then came the chance to finish his playing days in the razzmatazz of the US Soccer League and to dazzle a brand new collection of fans as he turned out for New York Cosmos. 'From Newport County to New York Cosmos – quite a culture shock,' laughs Harold.

But despite enjoying the experience and picking up around three times the wages he'd been on back in England, Harold got homesick and decided to go back to 'Blighty'. 'I must have done OK, the club got Pele to replace me!' he points out.

Back home, Harold had a couple of seasons at Mangotsfield, then became manager of Portway Bristol, taking them out of the Suburban League and into the Western League.

A call to return to his beloved Rovers in any capacity was one that Harold was never going to refuse. So in 1978, when manager Bobby Campbell asked him to become youth team coach, he jumped at it. Taking to the position like a duck to water, Harold was responsible for a batch of talented youngsters coming through the ranks. 'I shall always be grateful to Bobby Campbell,' says Harold.

By December 1979, Second Division Rovers were staring at a relegation fight and the Board decided it was time for a change. Campbell stepped down, returning to his old role of chief scout, and the board gave the job to Harold for the remainder of the season with his brief being to 'keep them up'.

Harold achieved the target he'd been given but it was a body blow for him when, at the end of the season, he was relieved of his managerial duties and Terry Cooper was duly appointed.

Bitterly disappointed, Harold walked away from Rovers, taking up the post of chief scout with Blackburn Rovers. In the following years he also scouted for Manchester City and Oxford. With blue blood flowing through his veins though, he again answered the call from Rovers in the 1980s, with newly installed player/manager David Williams wanting him back as youth team coach. So Harold was back. Sadly though, it was all over again in 1986 when Rovers, desperate to reduce their costs, made him redundant.

Not one to sit and mope, Harold spent five years looking after Norwich City's junior side and ran a centre of excellence for youngsters in Wales before retiring.

Married to Penny for over forty years, the couple have three sons and four grandchildren.

Left: It's another goal for Harold Jarman at Bristol Rovers.

Below: Harold today, looking after the garden at his Westbury home.

BOBBY JONES

Bobby Jones is unlikely to forget his first senior game for Rovers. Not only did he score a couple of goals, he was playing against a Middlesbrough team that had Peter Taylor in goal and Brian Clough at centre forward – later to go on to become the best managerial double act in the country.

'I certainly remember that day alright,' said Bobby. 'We won five-nil, I got a couple of goals and Cloughie didn't get a look in.' What you might call a perfect start for a man who went on to notch up over 470 senior games for The Pirates.

Cousin of Rovers colleague Joe Davis, Bobby's footballing career began as a pro in 1957. 'Most of my Rovers career was spent with Bert Tann as the boss. He was an excellent manager, a good talker and commanded respect,' said Bobby.

Although he preferred to play as an inside forward, Bobby was more often than not chosen to play on the left wing, where his pace on the ball would often leave opposing defenders floundering. He also appeared at centre forward and even at right-back. A firm crowd favourite with blue blood in his veins, many thought Bobby would always be at Eastville wearing the blue and white quarters of Rovers. Sadly, football is not like that, and when in 1966 a cash-strapped Rovers received a bid of £17,000 from Second Division Northampton Town, Bobby, somewhat reluctantly, was on his way.

Not surprisingly, Bobby never really settled at Northampton, and after just 18 appearances, got a move nearer home to Swindon Town. Even then he wasn't truly happy and after a mere 11 senior games for the Wiltshire club, Bobby gladly headed 'home' to rejoin Rovers for a £6,000 fee, less than a year after departing.

'I had another six years at Rovers, which was great,' said Bobby, whose final goal tally for The Pirates totaled 110. 'There wasn't another ground like Eastville in the country,' he reflected. Bobby's last senior game in Rovers colours was a cup match against Wolverhampton Wanderers at Molineux.

After leaving his beloved Rovers in 1973, Bobby turned out for Minehead in the Southern League for a couple of seasons, then joined Paulton as player/manager. He moved on to manage Bath City for six years, and also had spells as assistant manager at Forest Green Rovers, and manager at Mangotsfield and Oldland.

But the cut-throat world of football management could never replace those happy days playing for Rovers. Now sixty-eight, Bobby is retired and lives in the Kingswood area of Bristol with his wife Sandra. They have two sons, Mark and Neil.

Left: Bobby Jones on the ball for Rovers.

Below: Bobby today.

VAUGHAN JONES

If you had to pick a Rovers line-up of players that had blue blood in their veins it would be very difficult not to find a place for Vaughan Jones. In two separate spells with The Pirates he clocked up 437 starts for the side, and his ability to lead by example saw him take on the captain's armband during his second spell with the club, leading the club to promotion and an appearance in the Leyland Daf final at Wembley.

Born in Tonyrefail in Glamorgan, Vaughan was spotted playing for his local village team by a Rovers scout. Signing full-time professional forms in 1976, Vaughan's first manager was Don Megson. Before the end of his time with Rovers, he would play for another eleven managers as the manager's chair at the club became the proverbial hot seat. 'They were all interesting guys, but the best for me was Gerry Francis,' he said.

The tough-tackling defender had established himself as a regular in the side, playing mainly at right-back. So it came as something of a surprise when manager Bobby Gould decided to release him in 1982. Vaughan moved back home to Wales, where he had two seasons and around seventy games for Newport County (then in the Football League), before moving on for a spell at Cardiff City.

It was former teammate David Williams, who had succeeded Gould in the manager's chair at Rovers, who decided to strengthen the side by bringing Vaughan back to the club in December 1984, initially as a loan signing. An injury to Rovers' regular centre half opened the door of opportunity, and Vaughan took the chance with both hands to re-establish himself in the team's line-up.

When Gould returned to Rovers Vaughan kept his place, and two years later Gerry Francis breezed into the club as they embarked on one of their most successful periods. 'Gerry was very good for me and he asked me to be the side's skipper, which I was proud and delighted to be,' said Vaughan.

With the Francis revolution gathering momentum, Vaughan had the honour of leading his side out at Wembley, where they lost 2-1 to Tranmere Rovers and also to the Third Division championship. 'Wonderful times,' summed up Vaughan.

But, as is the cruel fate of football, those good times can't last for ever, and a broken leg suffered in a home match with Oxford kept him out of the game for well over a year, and that was the start of the end. 'I was never quite the same player after that and realised it was time to call it a day,' said Vaughan.

After quitting the professional game in 1993, Vaughan, like a lot of his former colleagues, worked as a financial advisor for eight years. These days he is tenant liaison officer, overseeing the need for central heating systems for council tenants.

Above: Vaughan in action for Bristol Rovers.

Right: Vaughan Jones today.

PHIL KITE

Former shot-stopper Phil Kite agrees that he's still Bristol Rovers through and through. Which is hardly surprising, considering that his dad took him to watch The Pirates from the age of five; that he went on to play 118 games for the club; that his sons Chris and Alex are on Rovers' books and that he is the club physiotherapist.

Having represented England Schoolboys, Phil joined Rovers as an apprentice in 1979, signing full-time professional forms a year later. He made his debut in an FA Cup tie with Preston – a game he's unlikely to forget:

> It was blowing a gale and, with the wind in our favour, we were four up at half-time. I thought to myself that this first-team goalkeeping's a doddle. It all changed in the second half though. With Preston now having the wind behind them, they laid siege to our goal. It was like the Alamo, but we clung on to win 4-3.

Phil went on to make his League debut at Derby the following week and by 1981, the year he was capped for England Youth, he had claimed the first-team jersey and became an ever-present.

The first of Phil's many loan transfers came about in early 1984. He'd lost his place in the side to Ray Cashley and was pleasantly surprised that Spurs needed goalkeeping cover due to injuries. The following year, Southampton paid Rovers £50,000 for Phil's services, although he had to play second fiddle there to Peter Shilton and played just five games. A loan move to Middlesbrough looked promising, but a shoulder injury resulted in a year out of the game.

After getting back to fitness, Phil moved on, signing for Gillingham in 1987. After 70 games for 'The Gills,' he was off to Harry Redknapp's Bournemouth for a fee of £270,000 plus Cherries forward Gavin Peacock. A year on he was off again, this time to Sheffield United and over the next sixteen months had loan spells at Mansfield, Plymouth, Rotherham, Crewe and Stockport:

> One of the funny things about me and Rovers is, although I played over 100 games for them, I never played for them at Twerton Park. But I did play against them there a few times.

In July 1993, Phil signed for Cardiff City, making 29 appearances before the most remarkable of his many transfers – to Bristol City:

> When I signed for City I rang one of my best mates at Rovers – Ian 'Ollie' Holloway. I said there's good news and bad news. The good news is I'm coming back to Bristol. Ollie asked what the bad news was. I said, I'm signing for City. Ollie hung up!

Phil was to spend two seasons at City, earning the affectionate nickname 'Gashead' from his teammates. But surgery for a prolapsed disc spelt the end of Phil's playing days: 'I desperately wanted to stay in the game, so I studied physiotherapy for four years, got my degree and got the vacant physio's job at Rovers', he said.

Married to Flora, the couple live in the Westbury-on-Trym area. In addition to their two footballing sons, they also have a daughter.

Left: Goalkeeper Phil Kite in action at Twerton Park AGAINST Rovers.

Below: Phil the physiotherapist, busy in the treatment room.

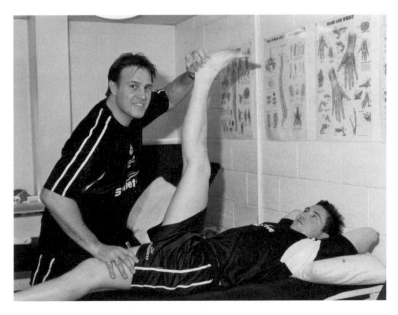

DAVID LEE

Former England Under-21 international Dave Lee was born in the Kingswood area of Bristol. He grew up a Rovers fan, but found fame at Stamford Bridge, before returning home in the later stages of his career to play for the club he'd supported as a boy.

'I joined Chelsea as a young lad in 1986,' recalled Dave. A midfielder or central defender, Dave made his debut for the club in 1988, scoring in the game against Leicester City. He went on to make over 200 appearances for Chelsea, scoring more than a dozen goals. He appeared in two League Cup semi-final matches for the club – against Sheffield Wednesday and Manchester United – and was also a member of the squad that won the Second Division Championship in 1988/89.

'I was very lucky to play alongside some fantastic players such as Glenn Hoddle, Ruud Gullit and Mark Hughes,' recalled Dave. He also lined up alongside 'some of the greats' after selection for the England Under-21s. 'There were some excellent players – Alan Shearer, Lee Sharpe, the Wallace brothers… really top-class footballers,' said Dave, who totalled 11 appearances alongside the cream of the young English talent.

A broken leg kept the Bristolian out of action for a year, and he had loan spells at Reading, Plymouth, Portsmouth and Sheffield United, before, in December 1998, he joined the club that he cheered on from the terraces as a lad.

'I came to Rovers around Christmas time and made my debut in a three-nil win at Colchester,' said Dave. Playing in midfield for The Pirates, Dave made his home debut in a 4-3 defeat to Burnley, although he did get on the scoresheet and followed that up by being in the side that had a resounding 6-0 win at Reading.

Less than a year after 'coming home', Dave was off on his soccer travels once again. Spells at Crystal Palace, Hearts, Colchester and Exeter followed, and Dave won't need reminding that he was sent off twelve minutes into his Exeter debut! But, in the summer of 2000, Dave had an offer he simply could not refuse, the chance to move to the other side of the world:

I signed for Paramatta Power, based in Sydney, Australia, and absolutely loved it there. The lifestyle was fantastic. There were quite a few ex-pats there – lads like Joe Miller from Celtic and West Ham winger Stuart Slater – and the only reason I came back a couple of years later was because of contractual problems.

Returning home, Dave's clubs included Havant & Waterlooville, Forest Green Rovers and Yate, and he was delighted when Weston-super-Mare manager Frank Gregan invited him to be assistant manager at the club. He subsequently moved on to join the management team at Swindon Town.

Married to Michelle, the couple live in Downend.

Above: Dave Lee (arms raised) celebrates a Chelsea goal.

Right: Ready for another game, a recent photo of Dave.

GARY MABBUTT

There aren't too many footballers that you could say were really true ambassadors of the game. A few names such as Bobby Charlton, Stanley Matthews and Bobby Moore spring to mind. But a true ambassador of the sport, a household name respected throughout the game both home and abroad, who came from Bristol, that's Gary Mabbutt.

Gary notched up nearly 150 senior games for Rovers, had sixteen years at Spurs (eleven of them as captain), won 16 England caps and was awarded an MBE for his services to soccer. And yet Gary had a few mountains to climb to achieve all those things. To start with he had to follow in the footsteps of his father Ray, a Rovers stalwart who made almost 450 appearances for The Pirates. Then there was the shadow of his elder brother Kevin, considered initially to be the more likely of the two to be a 'superstar'. And to top it all, Gary had to come to terms with being diagnosed with diabetes, an illness that could have spelt the end of a career in professional football for many:

> When my condition was first diagnosed, the specialist said that professional football was not for me. So I went and saw another specialist, who said more or less the same thing. I carried on seeing specialists until one said that if I looked after myself, it could be possible to be a diabetic and play soccer.

It says much for Gary's determination and dedication that he did just that, with the 'medication' in his case being four self-administered insulin injections daily — something he still has to do to this day.

Gary's long and distinguished career kicked off when he signed up as an apprentice at Rovers in 1977. By 1978 he was knocking on the first-team door, and once he'd established himself in the senior side, there was no looking back. Just like his father, he played in a variety of positions for Rovers, but manager Terry Cooper soon recognised that a defensive slot alongside a centre half was his best position. By the end of the 1981/82 season Gary had clocked up 138 senior starts and was attracting the attention of scouts from the higher divisions. Tottenham Hotspur, alerted to the talents of the young defender, came in with an offer of £105,000 and Gary was on his way to White Hart Lane.

Gary's composed performances at the heart of the Spurs defence soon resulted in a call-up to the England team, and he made his international debut against West Germany at Wembley. In 1984 he was a member of the successful Spurs side that won the UEFA Cup and was the happiest man at Wembley when, as team captain, he lifted the FA Cup for the London side in 1991 when they beat Nottingham Forest.

In 1994 there was another proud moment for Gary and his family when he was awarded the MBE for his services to football. But one award that he wasn't expecting came when he was nabbed by Michael Aspel, and stood gobsmacked as Michael uttered those immortal words, 'Gary Mabbutt, This is Your Life.'

After an impeccable career, Gary bowed out of professional soccer. A variety of injuries and knocks had finally caught up with him and a fragmented knee cap signalled the end of his playing days. But while the soccer manager's chair was not on his agenda, having an active role in the game certainly was and still is today. He serves on the FA Disciplinary Committee, has his own sports development company and plays a key role as a member of the FA International Development Committee.

Living in Hertfordshire, Gary is married to Kathy and they have two children, Stephannie and Tabitha.

Right: FA Cup-winning Spurs captain Gary Mabbutt.
(Photo courtesy of the *Sunday Independent*)

Below: Visiting the British Army in Afghanistan.

RAY MABBUTT

'Mr Versatility' – that's former Pirate Ray Mabbutt. In nearly 450 senior games for Bristol Rovers, Ray played in every position on the field for Rovers – bar one. 'The only shirt I never wore was the no.5,' said Ray.

Ray had actually joined Rovers in 1956 as a right-winger. 'I was playing in a reserve game and switched to wing-half when one of my teammates went off injured,' explained Ray. He went on to excel in the position and was soon establishing himself in the senior side. 'It was a lucky break for me and probably saved my career, as I wasn't exactly setting the world alight out on the wing,' he admitted.

But while Ray agrees that he enjoyed that midfield role for The Pirates, he was always willing to switch to a different role when required for the sake of the team. He was once asked to fill in at centre forward and responded by netting six times in three outings, including a hat-trick away to Northampton Town.

But what about between the sticks? 'Oh yes, I had to put on the goalkeeper's jersey twice during games, the second time when poor Bernard Hall sustained a bad head injury against Middlesbrough, which finished his career,' said Ray. And was he any good as a goalie? 'Well, from memory, we drew both matches with me in goal and down to ten men (pre-sub days) so I couldn't have been that bad!'

Over his twelve years with Rovers, Ray experienced many ups and downs, notching up 437 senior starts and netting 28 goals. When it was time to leave his beloved Eastville, Ray completed his League career 'across the bridge' at Newport County, where he played 44 games and added another 14 goals to his record.

After the Football League, Ray continued to turn out for a variety of local non-League clubs, with Trowbridge Town, Bath City, Frome, Clevedon Town (where he was player-manager) Mangotsfield and Keynsham benefiting from his skill and experience. His last club was Harptree United in the North Somerset League, before he finally called it a day at the age of forty-eight.

Away from the game, Ray proved equally successful at carving out a career in financial planning. 'I was always conscious of needing a trade when football finished, so got involved in financial matters and insurance while I was still playing,' he said.

Married to Barbara, the couple live in Winford and have a daughter called Sally and five granddaughters. And, of course, no story about Ray Mabbutt would be complete without mention of his two talented sons Kevin and Gary. 'They didn't follow in father's footsteps, I think you'll find they overtook me,' he said proudly.

Opposite above: Proud dad Ray, with sons Gary (left) and Kevin.

Opposite below: Tea time for Ray.

MARK McKEEVER

A stylish left-winger, Mark McKeever continued Rovers' trend of having skilful flankmen such as Harold Jarman and the late Mike Barrett that Pirate fans have warmed to over the years.

Born in Derry, Mark first made his mark at Peterborough United. 'John Still, who later had a spell as Rovers assistant manager, was the Peterborough boss who signed me. He was followed by Barry Fry, who was quite a character,' said Mark.

Mark's wing skills were soon attracting the scouts to London Road, and in April 1997 he was off to the top flight, with United accepting a £500,000 offer from Sheffield Wednesday. 'I made my debut for Wednesday in a nil-nil draw with Chelsea, which went out live on Sky Sports – not a bad way to start.'

Mark had also caught the eyes of his country's selectors and he went on to gain 12 caps for the Eire Under-18s and four for the Under-21s. 'I played alongside Richard Dunne, Damien Duff, Alan Quinn and Stephen McPhail for Eire,' he recalled.

In December 1998 Mark began the first of his two loan spells with Rovers, making his debut as a second-half sub in Rovers' first ever League game against Manchester City, which was at Maine Road in front of a near 25,000 crowd. The following March he had a loan spell with Reading, but injuries restricted his League appearances on his return to Wednesday, who were relegated at the end of the 1999/2000 season.

In February 2001 the Irishman returned to Rovers, initially on loan, with a permanent transfer less than two months later. 'When I first came to Rovers, Ollie (Ian Holloway) was the boss and he was very good,' recalled Mark. 'Later it was Gary Thompson who signed me on a permanent basis and after him I played for Gerry Francis and Ray Graydon.'

But, with Rovers going through an extended bad patch, Mark was one of a number of players freed by the club and he joined Conference South side Weston-super-Mare. 'It was almost like home from home when I joined Weston, as a number of ex-Rovers played for the club – Jon French, Lewis Hogg, Billy Clark, Dave Gilroy and David Mehew,' pointed out Mark.

Off the field, Mark worked at Bristol International Airport for a while, before taking up a position coaching in the Weston-super-Mare FC Academy. Towards the end of last season he moved to Gloucester City and during the summer signed for Bath City.

Mark lives with his partner Jackie and their two daughters, Caitlyne and Ciara, in Weston-super-Mare.

Above: Mark McKeever (left) in action.
(Photograph courtesy of *Sheffield Star*)

Right: Mark today, relaxing before a game.

DAVID MEHEW

Being the last player to score a competitive goal at Eastville is David Mehew's claim to fame, after finding the net in a reserve fixture against Watford.

Spotted playing for East Berkshire County schoolboys by a Leeds United scout, David spent a year as an apprentice at Elland Road. 'Eddie Gray was the manager at that time, and although I never made the first team, I did score 29 goals in 35 games. But even that couldn't save me from the cost-cutting they were making at the time and I got released,' explained David. That was in 1985, but luckily for him, Rovers manager Bobby Gould acted on a recommendation and offered him a contract. 'Bobby took a chance on me and for that I'll always be grateful,' added David.

It was also Bobby who promoted David's nickname of 'Boris'. 'One or two people had said I looked like Boris Becker the tennis player, but once Bobby latched onto it the nickname stuck,' said David. After impressing in Rovers' reserves, David broke through into the first team and got an impressive return of 10 goals from 20 starts. Then Bobby left, Gerry Francis took over, and David's career took a dive as Francis preferred the pairing of White and Penrice up front.

'I was loaned out to Bath City and then Trowbridge, and although I didn't realise it to start with, it turned out to be just what the doctor ordered. I got a lot of goals, which is what every striker needs and my confidence returned,' he said. Benefiting from specialist coaching from Francis, David fought his way back into Rovers' first team, playing on the right side of midfield. He went on to make nearly 250 senior appearances, scoring 78 goals. It was his goal in the 1-0 victory over Notts County, that got them through to the Leyland Daf final at Wembley, Rovers' first ever appearance there. And although they lost 2-1 to Tranmere, the Rovers side, including David, made a second trip to the stadium five years later in 1995, losing out to Huddersfield in the Division Two play-off final.

'Although it was obviously very disappointing to lose, getting the chance to play at Wembley is something you never forget,' he said proudly. He is also, quite rightly, proud of being a regular member of the side that won the old Third Division championship in 1990, finishing as the club's top scorer with 18 goals. 'Now that was a very good side,' he said.

After nine years with Rovers, David left in 1995 to sign for Walsall. He was to enjoy the taste of promotion once again as The Saddlers finished runners-up in Division Two. Dropping out of the League, he went on to have spells with a number of non-League sides including Weston-super-Mare, Farnborough, Bath City, Forest Green Rovers, Clevedon, Paulton, Brislington and, more recently, Gloucester City.

These days David is a sales manager for a stationery company, looking after the needs of offices in the Bristol and Weston-super-Mare area. He lives in Frampton Cottrell with his wife Louise and they have two sons, Oliver and Thomas.

Above: Rovers on the attack at Tiverton Par, with David Mehew second from the right.

Right: David at work today.

WAYNE NOBLE

Most young professional footballers get ready for a new season hoping for that 'big break'. Wayne Noble started two successive pre-seasons with two big breaks. Not that he wanted either of them – a broken foot in one pre-season friendly, and, the very next summer, a broken tib and fib (leg to you and me):

Talk about lightning striking twice. The first break was against a local amateur side, the other when we were playing against Birmingham City, when I got whacked by Wayne Clarke.

Born in Bristol in 1967, Wayne, a skilful midfield player, was a former member of a very good England Youth squad that included Tony Adams and the late David Rocastle. Having joined Rovers as an apprentice in 1983, he made his debut in the Rovers first team the following year at the tender age of sixteen. 'We were playing Port Vale in what used to be called The Associate Members Cup, and our centre half, Mark Hughes, had to go off injured after twenty minutes or so, and I got the nod to go on,' recalled Wayne.

During his time at Rovers, Wayne played under David Williams and Bobby Gould. He went on to make a couple of dozen senior appearances, scoring one goal in a 2-2 draw with Newport County. He was one of thirty players – a club record – to play for Rovers that season.

After leaving Rovers in 1987, Wayne had a year with (then) non-League Yeovil Town. 'Although not in the League at that stage, Yeovil had a very good side and gave Queens Park Rangers a battle in the third round of the FA Cup at Huish, before going down three-nil,' he pointed out.

Gloucester City, then managed by former Rovers favourite Brian Godfrey, bought him from The Glovers and he spent five years with the club. He made over 160 appearances for them and was appointed team captain. 'I probably played the best football of my career at Gloucester,' said Wayne. After leaving Gloucester he had spells at Bath City and Clevedon Town.

Now living at Portishead with his wife Lisa, Wayne has tried a number of 'Civvy Street' jobs. These have included travel agent, pub manager and delivery driver, before he got the call to go back into soccer, coaching schoolchildren as part of Rovers' soccer in the community programme:

It's great to be back in football and I get a lot of pleasure from coaching the kids. Hopefully, some of them will get the breaks – although I wouldn't want them to have the same 'big breaks' that I suffered at the start of my career!

Left: Wayne in action during his Rovers days.

Below: Rovers man Wayne at The Memorial Stadium.

TERRY OLDFIELD

Next time you get into a taxi, check out the driver – it might just be former Rovers star Terry Oldfield. 'I became a cabbie after chatting to a neighbour who drove a taxi,' explained Terry. 'It's great. I'm my own boss, can pick the hours to suit me and get away to the golf club whenever I want.'

After completing National Service in 1960, Terry went on to make 144 senior starts for Rovers, scoring 11 goals. He made his debut against Sunderland in November 1960, and although he played a number of games as a centre forward, it was at right half that Terry was normally to be found. 'Bert Tann was Rovers manager and nothing happened at the club that he didn't know about,' recalled Terry. 'He was excellent.' Recalling his days as a Pirate, Terry said:

> The local derbies with City were always special occasions. Then there were the pre-season training sessions when we used to stay at Burnham-on-Sea, they were great for team bonding. Oh yes, there was the time we went to Old Trafford for a cup match. They had a forward line of Herd, Law, Charlton and Best. We lost and I think Denis Law got a hat-trick – but what a fantastic experience.

An all-rounder, Terry was a useful cricketer in the days when many footballers combined the two sports. 'I played for Somerset, but football was always my priority,' pointed out Terry, which was just as well for Rovers fans, as the end of the cricket season usually overlapped with the start of the football programme.

After nearly a century and a half of senior games and over six years as a pro with The Pirates, Terry moved on for a year with Wrexham:

> I was doing OK there and the manager made me captain. Then we played the Welsh Cup final against Cardiff City and I got caught by a really bad tackle, which finished my playing career. You expect to get injuries, but this tackle was deliberately late.

After Wrexham, Terry took up a coaching job with Bradford Park Avenue, then in the Fourth Division:

> Jack Rowley, who I'd played for at Wrexham was their manager, and that was probably one of the main reasons why I went there. It was a disaster. There were no facilities, no organisation and no money. It was no surprise to me when they folded and went out of the League.

After football Terry tried his hand at a variety of jobs, including working as a pub landlord, estate agent and auctioneer, before taking to the road as a cab driver. He lives in the Backwell area of Bristol.

Terry Oldfield (far right) in action for Rovers.

Terry off to collect another fare.

BRIAN PARKIN

Brian Parkin could have been forgiven for thinking he was on a hiding to nothing when he signed for Rovers. He'd been brought in to replace fans' favourite Nigel Martyn, who had just commanded a record transfer fee for a goalkeeper with a move to the top flight. But Brian soon won over the fans with his goalkeeping skills, which were vital in ensuring Rovers won promotion in his first season with them. 'I came to Rovers as part of the million-pound transfer deal that took Nigel to Crystal Palace,' said Brian. 'From Selhurst Park to Twerton Park, now that was a culture shock!'

Brian's career began at Oldham Athletic, who were managed by Joe Royle. 'Joe was a brilliant bloke and I made my League debut under him,' recalled Brian. After a handful of games for 'The Latics', Brian moved on to Crewe Alexandra, notching up 98 senior appearances. His sound performances there hadn't gone unnoticed and he moved up a couple of divisions when signing for Crystal Palace. During his two years there he played 20 times, but Palace were looking to sign Martyn, and Rovers were happy to cash in and get his replacement at the same time, 'Rovers fans were very good to me and took to me straight away,' went on Brian. 'There was a great team spirit at the club and a brilliant squad of players and I soon settled in.'

In addition to gaining promotion, there were also two trips to Wembley on the agenda for the Birkenhead-born keeper, although both games ended in defeat. 'We lost to Tranmere Rovers in the 1990 Leyland Daf final and then to Huddersfield in the Division Two play-offs in 1995. Getting to Wembley was a great achievement, but to lose both games, especially the play-off final, was very disappointing,' he admitted.

In 1996 Brian left Rovers to move on to Wycombe Wanderers, where he made 26 senior appearances. An unsuccessful spell at Wimbledon, where injury problems meant the move was a non-starter in terms of League appearances, plus one senior game as a non-contract player for Notts County followed, before he got an unexpected SOS. Rovers wanted him back. 'Ollie (manager Ian Holloway) wanted cover for the goalkeeper's position and I was happy to come back,' explained Brian.

What should have been a highly successful season, with Rovers leading the division for much of the year, turned into a disaster, as the side hit a terrible run of results to drop out of the automatic promotion places. In fact, their end-of-season slide meant that they had to win their last game of the season, away to relegated Cardiff, just to make the play-offs. Lee Jones, who'd been a regular in the Rovers goal, was dropped and Brian was called up to take over.

Ironically, what should have been a day for celebration, both for Rovers and for Brian – it was his last senior game for the club and ensured his place in the record books as making the most post-war appearances in Rovers' goal – ended in tears, as the side went down 1-0. 'After doing so well throughout the season, we were all gutted at the way it ended – a terrible disappointment,' he summed up.

These days Brian gets his pleasure coaching the youngsters at Team Bath. 'There is a tremendous set-up here at the university and the side have done really well,' said Brian proudly.

Above: Brian in goalkeeping action.

Right: Ready for a day's coaching at Bath University.

GARY PENRICE

Ironically, former crowd favourite Gary Penrice might never have played for Rovers, but for arch rivals Bristol City instead, as he was on City's books as a schoolboy. 'Absolutely true,' said Penny, as he is known to friends, colleagues and fans. 'In fact, both City and Rovers turned me down as a youngster and I went to play for Mangotsfield.' However, Rovers soon saw the error of their ways and signed up the forward on part-time terms in 1983, giving him his full debut in a Freight Rover game against Swansea in early 1985, a few months after he'd signed full-time for the club.

When Bobby Gould took over as manager he moved the skilful inside forward into a midfield role, where Penny would be outstanding one week and anonymous the next. It took the arrival of Gerry Francis in the hot seat in 1987 to get Penny back into the front line, where he was an ever-present, knocking in 18 League goals that season. The following season he continued to find the net, this time getting 20 in the League and Rovers fans soon realised that it would only be a matter of time before someone made an offer that 'selling club' Rovers couldn't refuse.

A half-a-million-pound cheque from Second Division Watford did the trick and Penny soon had a host of new fans cheering him at Vicarage Road. He enhanced his reputation there by scoring in five consecutive League matches and going on to net 17 goals for The Hornets, who then doubled their money by selling him to Aston Villa for a cool million.

The move to Villa was not a resounding success, but he recovered his form on moving to Queens Park Rangers, averaging a goal every fourth game in his eighty-plus starts for them, before, in the 1995/96 season, a second, not quite so spectacular spell with Watford

In 1997, to the delight of Rovers fans, Penny 'came home'. Conscious that at thirty-three his playing days were coming to an end, he took an active role in coaching and acting as assistant manager to Ian Holloway, although he still managed enough games to pass the 300 mark in a Rovers shirt.

A run of bad results that saw Rovers miss out on a play-off spot after leading the table for so long meant that Holloway's job was on the line, and when the directors made the ill-fated decision to dismiss 'Ollie', Gary Penrice walked away from the club as well.

When Holloway took over the managerial reins at QPR he quickly re-established his partnership with Penny, bringing him to Loftus Road as his number two, although boardroom politics during 2005/06 saw the duo leave the club. They have since been reunited at Plymouth Argyle, where Gary is chief scout.

Gary and his wife live in Acton Turville in South Gloucestershire and have three daughters.

Above: Gary Penrice shoots for goal.

Right: Off on another scouting mission, Gary Penrice today.

GEORGE PETHERBRIDGE

A Bristol Rovers career spanning sixteen years, just four games short of 500 senior appearances, and just eight goals away from a century – not a bad record for Devonport-born George Petherbridge, the 5ft 4ins winger who became an Eastville favourite. And yet, these achievements might never have happened if it hadn't been for a family tragedy. 'My mother died when I was just three years old, dad was away in China with the navy and so I left Plymouth to stay with my grandparents, who lived near Eastville Park,' explained George.

Having settled in the blue half of Bristol, George signed for Rovers in 1946, after being spotted as a teenager playing local amateur football. 'I'd always played at inside forward, but Rovers manager Brough Fletcher switched me to the wing and I never looked back, God bless him,' said George with a smile.

A move out onto the wing enabled George to use his undoubted ball control and ability to send inch-perfect crosses to maximum effect, with his fellow forwards reaping the benefit. He was also no slouch when it came to finding the back of the net himself, as visitors Torquay United would testify when he claimed four festive goals at Eastville, in December 1951. And he was a key player in Rovers' success at the end of the 1952/53 season, when The Pirates won the Third Division South championship: 'The old Rovers side had a wonderful team spirit and some very good players. Players like Jackie Pitt, Harry Bamford, Geoff Bradford and Alfie Biggs… wonderful times.'

After the departure of Brough Fletcher, the managerial reins were taken up by Bert Tann and George was to serve under Bert for ten years. 'Bert Tann was manager for the bulk of my career. He was a very good man who certainly knew his football.'

Despite his lack of inches, George could take care of himself on the pitch when the situation demanded and could also pack a fierce shot. His consistent match-winning performances were rewarded by the FA when he was chosen to play for an England Select XI, which included the likes of Bobby Robson and John Bond.

Sadly, George's last season at Bristol Rovers – the 1961/62 season – ended in relegation, and a young Harold Jarman, with more than a little encouragement and coaching from George, was ready to take over the no.7 shirt.

But what of George after Bristol Rovers? Well, he played non-League football for a while, managed Western League side Glastonbury for five or six years, was a sports master at Millfield, had a spell as groundsman at Wells Cathedral School, and also ran The Angel public house in Sherston and later The Tamar pub overlooking the river. 'I enjoyed that, it was a lovely spot and busy in the summer – but very quiet in the winter,' he said.

Now retired and in his late seventies, George lives with his wife Rita in their Glastonbury home. They have a son, two daughters and eleven grandchildren – enough to start their own football team.

Right: George Petherbridge during his Rovers days.

Below: George relaxing at home.

TONY POUNDER

You could say that Tony Pounder is possibly the most qualified footballer to 'hover' in the opposition's penalty area. Or, that there's probably no one better at 'flying' down the 'wing'. After all, the former Rovers winger started his working life at Westlands of Yeovil, and now that his playing days are over, he's back with them. 'It's back to where it all began and now I'm a team leader in the machine shop at Westlands,' said Tony.

But, of course, working at a world-leading aerospace company is just part of Tony's career. He was also a pacey winger for Weymouth Town, Rovers, Hereford United and Yeovil Town.

It was Tony's skills on the wing for Weymouth that caught the eye of Rovers' scouts, and manager Gerry Francis, who had the uncanny knack of spotting non-League talent that could make it at League level. He saw enough to convince his directors that the £10,000 fee Weymouth were asking would be money well spent. And so it proved. 'The best coach I ever had – top man,' was Tony's verdict, when asked about Gerry.

Between 1990 and 1994 Tony was to make 114 starts for The Pirates, scoring 12 goals in the process. Three of those goals came in consecutive matches – against Swindon, Middlesbrough and Barnsley:

> There were some pretty tough full-backs about in those days. Charlie Palmer of Notts County was one. He clouted me early on in one match, just to let me know he was there. I wouldn't have minded so much, but the ball was nowhere near at the time!

A recurring ankle injury problem restricted Tony's appearances during his fourth season at Rovers and they released him in 1994. 'I was due to sign for Bournemouth, but they were going through severe financial problems at the time and it all fell through,' revealed Tony.

The next two seasons Tony spent at Hereford United, who just missed out on promotion on both occasions. 'The first year we narrowly failed to get into the play-offs and the following season we lost in the semi-finals,' he said.

After Hereford, Tony had the chance to join Cardiff City, but instead opted for (then) non-League Yeovil Town:

> Graham Roberts was manager at the time and he offered me the chance to combine playing with coaching. This meant better prospects and a longer-term future and I had three happy years there. Also, coming from Yeovil, it was the perfect move for me.

Winding down his playing days, Tony played Western League football for a while before hanging up his boots. He lives in the Yeovil area with wife Andrea and young children Ben and Ellice.

Left: Tony Pounder (left) in action during his playing days.

Below: Time for a tea break, Tony today.

GRAEME POWER

Ask defender Graeme Power which team has the best fans in the country and he doesn't hesitate. 'There's no question about it – Bristol Rovers,' is his immediate response. 'I was only with the club for two seasons, but I soon found out that their fans are unique – the very best.'

Graeme started his soccer career on the youth training scheme with Queens Park Rangers in 1993, when Ian 'Ollie' Holloway was a player at the club. After signing as a full-time pro in 1995, Graeme was released a year later. But Ollie, by then in charge at Rovers, remembered the tough tackling left-back and brought him to the club.

'Ollie brought in myself and two other lads - Matt Lockwood and Steve Parmenter – from QPR,' recalled Graeme. But competition for the no.3 shirt was fierce. 'Apart from me, there was Matt and also former Man United defender Lee Martin battling it out for the left-back spot,' he pointed out.

Apart from the competition for his position, Graeme also lost a large part of his two seasons at Rovers through injury. 'I dislocated my shoulder in a game against Plymouth and was out for the best part of seven months,' he recalled.

Injuries and fierce competition for the full-back position meant Graeme only made 26 appearances for the club and Rovers released him in 1998. Graeme moved down the road to Exeter City, going on to make 165 starts for The Grecians. 'I enjoyed my time at Exeter,' he said. 'I settled well in the area and I found Steve Perryman to be an excellent coach.'

Unfortunately the club was going through a well-documented cash crisis and when they lost their League status, Graeme decided to call it a day at St James' Park. 'The club was going through a very difficult time – in deep trouble financially and getting relegated from the Football League. I always knew that there would come a time when I would leave full-time football and I felt that this was that time,' he revealed.

Short spells at Tiverton and Weymouth followed, before Graeme signed for Southern Premier League side Bath City. He left Tiverton Park at the end of last season to sign for Westen League high-flyers Truro City. Having already decided on getting a career outside of soccer, Graeme is currently taking a four-year course at Exeter University, to obtain a teaching degree in physical education. 'It's something I've wanted to do for some time,' pointed out Graeme, who lives in Paignton with his partner Kim. 'I had ten years as a professional footballer, but, when the time came, I was quite happy to get out of full-time soccer,' he summed up. 'But those Rovers fans – different class.'

Left: Graeme during his time at Rovers.

Below: A recent pre-match photo of Graeme.

PHIL PURNELL

When it comes to injuries, some players are lucky and go through their careers practically unscathed, while others spend more time on the treatment table than on the pitch. Well, the gods certainly weren't smiling on former Rovers winger Phil Purnell, when it came to going easy on the injury front. So much so, that he finally had to call it a day as far as a football career was concerned, at just twenty-eight years of age.

To list some of the injuries that Phil (or Percy as he was known by fans and teammates alike) had to overcome would probably make those of a squeamish nature feel faint. Broken legs, pelvic problems, cartilage trouble, ligament damage... you name it, Percy's had treatment for it. But, despite suffering practically every footballing ailment known to man, he always put on a brave face and got on with getting fit and playing, which earned him the admiration of the fans and the respect of opposing full-backs.

Percy had joined Rovers as a schoolboy at the age of ten. Even at that tender age he'd had a few injuries and gave the game up for a while. After finishing school, and disappointed not to be offered an apprenticeship by Rovers, Percy went to work as an apprentice at British Aerospace and later joined his father in the furniture retail business. He was also turning out for Western League side Mangotsfield United, a well-respected local club which had an excellent record for producing football stars. His dazzling wing displays convinced Rovers they wanted him back and he signed up, initially as a part-timer, in 1984.

Following in a long line of talented Rovers wingers, Percy was soon delighting the fans with his skills down the left flank. Not the tallest of players, what Percy lacked in height, he more than made up for with skill and commitment. By the time that Rovers had left their spiritual home at Eastville for Bath's Twerton Park, Percy had made a strong case for making the no.11 shirt his own.

Percy was not a prolific goalscorer. During his time at Rovers he found the net 22 times but, more often than not, those goals were vital. It was his goal at Newport County (the only goal of the game) at the end of the 1986/87 season which saved Rovers from relegation to the Fourth Division. The following year he played all but five games, netting eight times in the process, and twelve months later he played a major role in helping to get The Pirates to the play-offs.

Although Rovers' defeat to Port Vale in the play-offs at the end of that season was a disappointment, success was only round the corner, and Percy thoroughly deserved his 1989/90 Third Division Championship medal, scoring the first of three Rovers goals at Blackpool to send Rovers up. 'Looking back, of the goals I got in my Rovers career, the ones at Newport and Blackpool were certainly the most important,' summed up Percy.

But, at a time when talented wingers were much in demand, injuries continued to blight Percy's career. A relatively meaningless reserve match against Yeovil Town resulted in another broken leg and this time there was no way back.

Married to Kerry, with a teenage daughter and eleven-year-old son, Phil now works as a financial advisor.

Above: Phil 'Percy' Purnell in Rovers action.

Right: Phil at work today.

HOWARD RADFORD

After eleven seasons as custodian between the sticks at Bristol Rovers, Howard Radford decided to call time on his football career. So it seems only natural that for the next eighteen years he regularly called 'time' – in his capacity as a pub landlord:

> It was the end of the 1961/62 season and we'd just been relegated to the Third Division. I'd signed on for the next season, gone home, thought about the injuries I'd been carrying and the possibility of perhaps losing my place in the first team and decided that it was time to call it a day.

Born in Abercymon in South Wales, Howard played representative football for the army during his National Service. His eleven seasons at Rovers began in 1951 after he was spotted by scout Wally Jennings playing for Penrhiwceiber in the Welsh League. 'We were bottom of the table and always struggling but it meant, as a goalkeeper in a struggling side, you were always kept very busy'.

> They had a very good side at Eastville and Geoff Bradford was an exceptionally gifted player. And Peter Hooper – what a shot he had. Then there was Josser Watling, the club's 'joker,' – you had to watch out for him!

Those were good years for The Pirates. Promotion to the Second Division, big crowds home and away, and a fine one-for-all team spirit:

> I always loved playing in front of big crowds. The atmosphere is totally different than a half empty stadium or if you are playing in a reserve match. My favourite away ground was Anfield. There was always something very special about going to play at Liverpool. I loved playing there. We always seemed to do well at Liverpool and the atmosphere in the ground was fantastic.

Of course, in Howard's time, goalkeepers didn't get the protection that they do today. 'We used to take a few knocks and I don't think I had a single season without having to miss a few games through injury,' said Howard. 'In fact, when I quit football, I'd been carrying a knee injury for a couple of seasons.'

After finishing at Rovers, Howard went into the licensing trade, running the Chequers public house in Old Market Street for eighteen months, The Ring of Bells at Coalpit Heath for nearly five years and, finally, The Bishop Lacey Inn at Chudleigh in Devon, which he ran for eleven-and-a-half years and where he still helps out behind the bar, following his retirement. 'I've also driven a bread lorry, delivered bananas and worked with people with learning difficulties,' added Howard.

Married to Shirley, Howard has four children from his first marriage, twelve grandchildren and a great-grandchild. 'Do you know,' said Howard, 'Some people say you have to be mad to be a goalkeeper… they're probably right!'

Right: Howard in goalkeeping action for Rovers.

Below: Howard, on a recent return trip to Rovers.

PAUL RANDALL

When striker Paul Randall finally hung up his boots, it was just what the doctor ordered for defenders in the Somerset Senior League, where the former Rovers star had been winding up his playing days. And if anyone knows anything about 'what the doctor ordered' it's Paul – he's a chemist at a pharmacy in Somerton, 'I started off as a driver for the pharmacy about thirteen years ago and was encouraged to study as a chemist, took the two-year course and here I am.'

As a teenager, Paul combined working in a supermarket with playing non-League football for Glastonbury, where he was soon knocking in the goals. 'Former Rovers winger Georgie Petherbridge, who was the Somerset County Under-18s manager, had recommended me to Rovers and, after scoring against them in a pre-season friendly, I was on my way to Eastville,' recalled Paul.

Rovers' fans soon took to the affable scouser, and his ratio of 20 goals from his first 28 games was a major factor in the club avoiding relegation from the Second Division at the end of the 1977/78 season.

By the start of the following season Paul's goalscoring ability was attracting the scouts. Never a club who could afford to keep their best players, Rovers accepted a Christmas offer of £175,000 from Stoke City and Paul was on his way to The Potteries. 'Some people say it didn't really work out for me at Stoke, but I helped them gain promotion to the top division and enjoyed my time there,' he told me.

By January 1981, Rovers were struggling at the bottom of the Second Division table and manager Terry Cooper brought the terrace hero back home for £55,000, with Rovers supporters actually putting their hands in their pockets to make a contribution towards the transfer fee. 'I'd always had a good rapport with the Rovers fans, they were fantastic to me and it was good to come home,' said Paul. Despite his welcome return after a two-year exile, Paul took time to settle back in and Rovers were unable to avoid dropping down to the Third Division.

Paul was to spend another five years with The Pirates, scoring 106 goals in 255 full appearances altogether, but in 1986 he was released by Bobby Gould and he signed for Yeovil Town. 'I had three or four years at Huish and helped them gain promotion to the Conference,' Paul said. After Yeovil came four seasons at Bath City, where, in one season, he scored 51 goals to overtake the record previously set by Twerton Park legend Charlie 'Cannonball' Fleming. Next was a short spell at Weymouth, followed by Clevedon Town, Welton Rovers, Glastonbury, Street and finally Wells.

Living with his Italian-born wife Filomena in picturesque Wells, the couple have a teenage son Mark, who plays soccer at county level, and a young daughter Kelly, an accomplished county netball player.

Opposite above: Scoring for Rovers at Eastville.

Opposite below: On dispensing duty at the Moss Pharmacy.

ANDY REECE

You would think after a football career that included nearly 300 games for Rovers, Andy Reece would be looking forward to a rest. In fact, 'arrest' is the right word, for Andy Reece is now a detective with the West Midlands Constabulary. 'I was looking for a new career when my playing days were coming to an end, applied for a job with the police force and got it,' explained Andy.

A central midfield player, Andy was one of a number of players that Rovers (then) manager Gerry Francis astutely spotted playing non-League football – in Andy's case, Dudley Town – and successfully brought into League football at Rovers. 'I came to Rovers in 1987 and was made to feel very welcome as soon as I arrived,' said Andy. 'It was a completely new challenge in my life and I was determined to make the best of it.'

Rovers' fans soon took to the hardworking central midfielder and the feeling was mutual. 'Rovers fans were always very good to me and they're certainly the best that I've ever played for,' he said.

Such were his displays for The Gas that the year they won the Third Division championship, he missed just three games. Twerton Park became Fortress Twerton during that season, and for the first time in the club's history, they were unbeaten in the League at home. 'That was certainly the highlight of my time at Bristol and the supporters certainly deserved that success,' he pointed out.

After Francis left the club, Andy played under Martin Dobson and then Malcolm Allison. 'Malcolm Allison was certainly one of football's characters,' said Andy with a smile. 'You don't get managers like Malcolm in the game anymore, which is such a pity as the game needs characters like him.'

Between 1987 and 1993, Andy clocked up 272 senior starts, plus 12 as sub for Rovers. During that time he contributed 23 goals from his deep midfield role. Andy also had a loan spell at Walsall, where he played 15 times, before moving on to Hereford United. He stayed at Edgar Street for three years, playing another 71 League games. Teammates in the Hereford side included former Rovers players Tony Pounder and Steve White, and from the red half of the city, Andy Llewellyn.

Now living in Birmingham, Andy has been with the police force for eleven years and has played soccer in the West Midlands and English police force teams. Married to Jane, the couple have a daughter and two sons. 'My kids still watch me play in old Rovers videos that I've got,' said Andy. 'The only trouble is they're all in black and white!'

Right: Andy Reece during his time at Rovers.

Below: 'Ello, 'ello, 'ello – Andy Reece today.

BILL ROOST

There's so much you could write about Bill Roost – and he's certainly got some good stories to tell – that you could probably devote a whole book to him, never mind one page. Yet Bill's big breakthrough in football came later than most:

> I was playing for Stonehouse in the old Western League. A Rovers scout invited me to have a trial match with them. When he asked how old I was and I told him I was twenty-five, he said it would be better if I knocked a couple of years off my age and make it twenty-three – and that's what he put on his paperwork!

Within a week of playing in a reserve match against Coventry and scoring in a 1-1 draw, Bill became a fully fledged professional footballer with The Pirates. Brough Fletcher was the manager at the time, and Bill got to make his League debut in a Good Friday match with Reading. He put in a sterling performance but also took a nasty knock in the face for his trouble:

> I was due to turn out for the reserves at Arsenal the next day, but in the morning my mouth had swelled up from the knock and I really didn't feel up to playing. I went to the ground in the morning and I told Mr Fletcher. He said I should go home and get some rest – but to make sure I was back at the ground at one o'clock, because he wanted me in the first team!...
> After Brough Fletcher came Bert Tann – an excellent manager who knew how to get the best out of his players. Not long after he took over, he told me I'd never make a centre forward and switched me to inside forward – and he was right, the switch really improved my game.

Soon to become a crowd favourite who never gave less than 100 per cent, Bill went on to clock up 198 senior games between 1948 and 1959, notching 52 goals in the process. He also became the players' official union rep.

After eleven years at Rovers, Bill moved on to spend two years under Bert Head at Swindon Town. 'That was the worst thing I ever did,' he admitted. 'The move didn't work out at all and to say that me and the manager didn't get on would be something of an understatement.'

After his ill-fated move to Swindon, Bill returned to non-League football, finishing his playing days at Minehead. For a while he worked with former teammate and close friend Josser Watling on the commercial side at Rovers. He ran the Black Horse public house in St George for five years, before finishing his working days on the docks at Avonmouth.

Now in his eighties, Bill, who is a widower, lives in the St George area of Bristol.

Left: On the ball during his playing days.

Below: Bill today.

CARL SAUNDERS

You could say that life has come full circle for fans' favourite Carl Saunders. He has gone from cult hero among Gasheads as one of the boys in blue (and white) with Rovers, to working with the boys in blue at the Avon & Somerset Constabulary, where he is Community Liaison Officer:

> My role with the constabulary involves addressing diversity issues and liaising with and supporting local communities. Being an ex-pro footballer helps break down barriers when I'm working in the community.

Born in Birmingham in 1964, Carl was spotted playing for the West Midlands county side by a Stoke City scout and, after trials, signed professional forms in 1982. 'The manager there at the time was Ritchie Barker and I shall always be grateful to him for giving me my chance,' said Carl.

A versatile player who often operated at full-back and midfield, Carl made 164 appearances for The Potters, but, following management changes at the club, Carl decided to move on and Rovers came in with a bid of £70,000. 'I could have gone to City or Notts County, but Gerry Francis 'sold' the club to me and it turned out to be a great move,' said Carl, who signed for Rovers in February 1990.

Playing up front, where he replaced Gary Penrice (who had moved to Watford) Rovers fans soon took to the newcomer – a goal on his debut doing his Rovers credibility no harm – and they gave him the nickname Billy Ocean, because of his likeness to the pop singer of the same name. 'I still get called that today,' laughed Carl.

An ever-present in the side that won the (old) Third Division championship, Carl won the Man of the Match award in the Leyland Daf Trophy final at Wembley (Rovers losing 2-1 to Tranmere) and scored Rovers' consolation when they were narrowly beaten in an FA Cup tie at Anfield.

Carl enjoyed five seasons with Rovers, scoring 51 goals in his 162 appearances. A contractual dispute saw him leave Twerton Park, and after brief spells at Oxford, Middlesbrough and Walsall, he tried his luck overseas. 'I had a season with Sliema Wanderers in Malta, finishing as top scorer,' said Carl. 'It was a good standard of football and a great experience.'

On returning home, Carl was hoping to resurrect his career in Britain. Sadly, the injuries he suffered in a car accident put paid to those plans. Dedicated to helping youngsters with their problems and an ardent supporter of the fight against racism, Carl worked for Social Services for a while, before joining the local constabulary to take up the role of Community Liaison Officer. Of his time with Bristol Rovers, Carl said, 'The team spirit among the Rovers players was fantastic and in Gerry Francis the club had a great motivator and man manager. And I'll never forget the Rovers fans – absolutely brilliant.'

Carl celebrates another of his goals at Twerton Park.

These days Carl works in the community for the Avon & Somerset Constabulary.

JEFF SHERWOOD

If anyone knows about defence, it's former Rovers centre half Jeff Sherwood. For both the centre of defence and the Ministry of Defence have taken up much of his life. 'I joined the MOD in 1977 and even when I made the breakthrough and signed for Rovers, I signed as a part-timer,' said Jeff.

Jeff had been signed by Rovers in 1982, having been spotted playing for Stuart Taylor's Bath City – later to become Rovers' landlords. 'My first game for Rovers was against City, playing alongside the likes of Ollie (Ian Holloway) and Keith Curle,' recalled Jeff. 'What you might call a baptism of fire – and we won.' He went on to make his League debut at Preston North End.

Obviously playing part-time created its own problems, but Jeff managed to work to a timetable around both careers:

> I used to go in after work for coaching from John McDowell and if I was selected for the first team, the MOD let me take leave to attend Friday training and the team meeting. The MOD was very understanding and I've always appreciated that.

Under the management of Bobby Gould, Jeff played over twenty senior games for The Pirates. 'I enjoyed playing at Portsmouth – a nice ground – while on the other hand, Millwall was certainly an experience! When we played away I roomed with Mike Channon.' So did the former England international pass on any tips? 'Oh yes – the only trouble was they were all horse racing tips!'

In 1983 Bobby Gould left Rovers to manage his first club, Coventry City. Being a part-timer was always going to count against him and Jeff found himself surplus to requirements with the new manager. He returned to Bath City, then managed by another Rovers old boy, Bobby Jones, and had three seasons there, before being transferred to (then non-League) Yeovil Town.

In 1990, Gloucester City paid out £15,000 to sign the man from the MOD (a huge sum in non-League circles). 'It was a club record fee and not too long afterwards they went bust – but don't blame me for that,' pointed out Jeff. He returned to Yeovil in 1992, but injuries saw him out of the game for nine months. 'After that I had two spells with Clevedon Town, returned to Bath in between and also played for Salisbury. In 2000 I turned out for Brislington, which meant I'd played competitive football for four decades,' he declared proudly.

Married to Angela, who runs a florists business, the couple live in Hanham. They have a teenage son and two teenage daughters.

Above: Jeff (front row, far right) in a pre-season Rovers line-up.

Right: Jeff Sherwood today.

JAMIE SHORE

If guts, grit and determination were all that was needed, then Jamie Shore would still be gracing the football fields of England, probably in the top flight. Sadly though, guts, grit and determination were not enough to save the career of this talented midfield player, as he battled against serious injury. He had sixteen knee operations, including a pioneering cartilage transplant.

At the beginning, the future looked bright for the youngster from Backwell. Given a choice of City, Rovers, Arsenal, Manchester United, Southampton, Villa or Norwich, Jamie opted to sign for the latter. 'I had been on Norwich's books from the age of twelve and I was fortunate to travel all over Europe,' said Jamie.

After earning a full-time placement at the FA's National School at Lilleshall, Jamie established himself in the England Under-16 side, where his teammates included the likes of Stephen Clemence, Emile Heskey and Jamie Carragher. By the time he'd reached seventeen, he became the youngest player in Norwich's history to sign professional forms, progressing into the first-team squad. It was all going well – too well.

'I was playing in a youth game at Arsenal and was carried off in the first minute with a knee injury,' he recalled. Jamie went on to have nine operations over the next three years and it says much for the ability of the youngster that Rovers gave him a four-and-a-half year contract, as he looked to regain his fitness and relaunch his career. He made his debut for The Pirates in September 1998, coming on as a sub in a home match against Chesterfield.

Jamie went on to make 22 full appearances, plus seven as sub, scoring five goals in the 1998/99 season, but sadly it was to be one season only. Despite those countless operations, involving surgeons at home and in the United States, that knee injury just wouldn't go away, even with a new cartilage and Jamie had to give up. Phil Kite, Rovers physiotherapist, who spent hundreds of hours treating Jamie, commented:

I suppose it was always going to be a gamble, taking Jamie on with the knee problem when he first came from Norwich. We knew we had an immense talent on our hands but, after a hell of a lot of effort and trauma, he had to call it a day.

Former Rovers manager Ian Holloway continued:

Jamie is a smashing lad, but above all, one of the best players I have had the privilege of standing next to on a football pitch. It was one of the lowest points of my footballing career when he had to call it a day because he could have been the next Paul Gascoigne – he was that good.

Now living in Clifton with his partner Natalie and their dog Winston, Jamie has thrown himself into running his own very successful soccer academy. 'It's all about helping young soccer players achieve their full potential,' summed up Jamie. As to how far this genial, talented and determined individual could have gone in the game, we'll never know.

Left: Jamie in action for Bristol Rovers.

Below: Jamie today at his soccer academy.

TOM STANTON

When Rovers manager Fred Ford rang me one morning and asked me to sign for Bristol Rovers, I said I'd think about it. He rang again the next morning, and the next morning, and the morning after that, each time a little earlier than the day before – he just wore me down in the end!

And, in his own words, that's how Tom Stanton came to sign for Rovers.

Glasgow-born Tom began his soccer career as a sixteen-year-old at Liverpool. 'A football genius is the only way you could describe Bill Shankly,' summed up Tom. 'It was Bill who recommended me to Fred Ford years later.'

It was a blow to Tom when Liverpool released him and he returned to Scotland. He was training with Kilmarnock, when, to his surprise, Arsenal came in for him. 'I was actually Bertie Mee's first signing,' revealed Tom. 'The club treated me and my parents very well, inviting us down to London and looking after us.'

After making steady progress in the reserves, Tom was told he was going to be in the first team the coming Saturday. Sadly, he was injured playing for the reserves just a few days before his planned First Division debut and he was out of the game for nine months. 'By the time I'd recovered, Pat Rice had made the full-back position his own and I was loaned out to Mansfield Town,' explained Tom.

After a successful spell with The Stags, playing 37 games, Tom was offered a contract with the club, but wasn't overly keen on staying:

> That's when I got the calls from Fred Ford. I couldn't believe it when I first got to Bristol and went to Eastville Stadium – flower beds behind the goals and a greyhound track running round the pitch – I'd never seen a football ground like it. But I did grow to love the place and the supporters.

Between 1968 and 1976, Tom featured in nearly 200 games – one game short of the 200 in fact – and scored nine goals. A versatile player, he performed in both full-back positions, as well as midfield. He even became an emergency goalkeeper, pulling on the keeper's jersey when the late Dick Sheppard was injured during a game.

An ever-present in the 1973/74 promotion season, Tom left Rovers in 1976, having spells at Weymouth, Forest Green and Clevedon Town, where he was player/coach. He also helped out at Rovers, coaching the youngsters.

Away from soccer, Tom has worked in telecommunications. This resulted in him and a colleague breaking new ground by setting up the UK's first computerised call centre.

Married to Sue, the couple live in Nailsea. Tom has two children from his first marriage and three stepchildren.

Left: A lull in play for Tom during a Rovers game at Eastville.

Below: A communications expert these days.

DAVE STONE

Practically every member of the successful 1958 Bristol Boys team who were winners of the English Schools Trophy chose to go to Bristol City. One who didn't, but headed off to the other side of Bristol instead, was Dave Stone, who went on to play over 160 games for Rovers. 'There were some very good players in the Bristol Boys team, like Jantzen Derrick and Brian Clark. They all chose City, but I'd always supported Rovers, so I turned City down and went to Eastville instead,' said Dave, who now works on the purchase ledger of a care home charity, based at Westbury-on-Trym.

Having joined Rovers' ground staff as a sixteen year old, Dave progressed through the juniors, youth team and reserves, before making his first-team debut at Northampton Town in 1962: 'There were some great players in the Rovers side – Geoff Bradford, cousins Joe Davis and Bobby Jones and of course Alfie Biggs – an amazing player with a first-class attitude.'

As a young Rovers fan Dave studied The Pirates' skipper, right half Jackie Pitt. 'He was fantastic, the player I most admired, and yes, it would be fair to say that I modelled my game on him,' admitted Dave. And he was to learn a lot more from the maestro – Jackie was a coach at Rovers when Dave joined them as a youngster willing to learn.

As an old fashioned right half, Dave didn't get too many goals – eight in all, during his time with Rovers, but he vividly remembers two of them:

> We went to Bournemouth for an FA Cup tie and weren't expected to win, but I got the first goal in a 3-1 victory. The FA Cup was kind to me because the following season we played away at Walsall and I scored again – and we won.

In 1968 Dave bade farewell to Eastville, joining Southend United on a free transfer. 'I had six months there and, to be honest, it just didn't work out,' said Dave. After Southend came a spell as player/manager at Hastings United in the old Southern League, before he headed back to the south west. Over the following years Dave had successful spells playing or managing – often combining both roles – at Glastonbury, Welton Rovers, Portway Bristol and Clevedon Town.

Off the football field Dave enjoyed thirty-three years working in the offices of an engineering firm, before being made redundant. Never one to remain idle, Dave found employment in the finance office of St Monica Trust.

Married to Margaret for over forty years, the couple live in Rudgeway. They have two sons, Gerry and Robin and a young granddaughter, Emilia.

There is an interesting postscript to our story. Dave's playing days aren't quite over. Never shy to start a sing-song on those long coach journeys to away games, he is now a member of the local parish players, performing musicals such as *South Pacific* and *Guys and Dolls*.

Opposite above: Dave Stone (centre) clears under pressure in an FA Cup match at Eastville.

Opposite below: A matter of trust for Dave Stone today.

NICK TANNER

From Mangotsfield to Anfield to Horfield (with a time at Eastville in between), that's the travel log of Bristol-born defender Nick Tanner. 'To step up from Mangotsfield to Rovers was great, but to then move on to Liverpool was fantastic,' said Nick.

Nick was spotted by Rovers scout and former star Harold Jarman playing for Western League side Mangotsfield United. 'Ralph Miller was Mangotsfield's manager at the time and the club produced some great local talent – Gary Smart, Percy Purnell and Gary Penrice for example,' he pointed out. After signing for The Pirates, Nick put on a first-team shirt for The Pirates in May 1985, when he came on as a sub in the old Gloucestershire Cup final between City and Rovers. He promptly scored from fully forty-five yards to help Rovers to a 3-1 win. He made his League debut the following August against Darlington, going on to make over 100 appearances in Rovers blue and white quarters. 'There were some very good players at Rovers and a great sense of camaraderie. Trevor Morgan and Vaughan Jones were good players on the park and good mates off it.'

In July 1988, Nick said goodbye to his Bristol teammates and headed for Anfield, after Rovers had accepted a £20,000 bid for his services. 'Actually, I had the choice of Liverpool or Torquay United,' said Nick. 'What you might call an easy decision to make. Going to Anfield was one of my better decisions.'

During his time at mighty Liverpool Nick made over sixty senior appearances, plus four as sub. His memories include scoring in a Merseyside derby with arch rivals Everton, as well as playing against Rovers in a fourth round FA Cup match at Twerton Park (which finished in a draw) and the subsequent replay – Liverpool winning 2-1.

With competition for places in the Liverpool line-up fierce, Nick had loan spells at Norwich and Swindon Town. And apart from the battle for places, Nick was also battling a recurring back injury, which refused to go away. 'Basically it was a football wear and tear injury. They tried everything – acupuncture, injections, a chiropractor, but all to no avail.'

And so it was in 1994 that at just twenty-nine Nick was forced to quit the professional game. He returned to his roots at Mangotsfield, where he had a two-year spell as manager, followed by a short period managing Welton Rovers. He went on to manage Hellenic League side Almondsbury Town and is currently manager of Gloucester County League side Worron Rovers.

Nick, who is a new business account manager for a firm of insurance brokers based at Chippenham, lives in the Bradley Stoke area of Bristol and has a twelve-year old son (William) from his previous marriage. Summing up his football career, Nick said, 'I had ten years – ten brilliant years – doing what most lads can only dream of.'

Opposite above: Nick in his Rovers days – middle row, fourth from the right.

Opposite below: Late tackles are one thing, but Nick (second left) turning up late for work is another.

STUART TAYLOR

At 6ft 5ins in his stockinged feet, Stuart Taylor was the tallest player in Rovers' history, an advantage when you play as a central defender. He also holds the club record for playing the most senior games – 620 altogether, having signed on as a part-time professional in 1965. 'I was training to be a plumber at the time and wanted to complete my apprenticeship before signing full-time for Rovers,' explained Stuart.

When the affable defender made his League debut at Workington in 1966, the nineteen year old could not possibly have forseen that he would go on to become a pillar of the Rovers defence for the best part of fourteen years. 'In those days most teams travelled away by train, so, after playing at Workington, we got back into Bristol Temple Meads around three in the morning. I was up and off plumbing at eight-thirty,' he recalled.

By the 1968/69 season Stuart was forming a solid central defensive partnership with Larry Lloyd. An ever-present for four successive seasons, Taylor enjoyed moving up for corners and free-kicks, which brought him 34 goals between 1966 and 1980. He was also proud at being asked to take on the role of team captain. 'Yes, I enjoyed being skipper and considered it a privilege to lead the side out,' he said.

Looking back on his career, two of the highlights were undoubtedly winning the Watney Cup in 1973 and then gaining promotion from the Third Division the following season. 'That was the best Rovers side I played in,' he admitted. 'There were some very good individual players and as a team we were very hard to beat.'

As well as being the tallest player to play for Rovers and having the record for the most senior appearances, Stuart also just missed out on a third achievement – the greatest number of consecutive appearances:

I was an ever-present for four or five seasons and was only a few games behind the late Ray Warren's record, which I think was 264 consecutive games. Just when I thought I would overtake that, I got sent off and had to serve a one-match suspension.

When Stuart finally called it a day with Rovers, he took on the role of player/manager at nearby Bath City. The team had been going through a bad time and had been bottom of the Conference. 'In my first season there we finished sixth and the second year we came third,' he said proudly. 'Then the directors decided that the manager's job should be a part-time position, which was ridiculous, so I left.'

After Bath City, Stuart saw out his playing days with Cadbury Heath, continuing to turn out for them until well into his fifties. 'I tried my hand at a few things after football, but plumbing has always been my real trade and I enjoy it, so that is what I do today,' he said.

Left: Stuart Taylor jumps highest for the ball.

Below: Working today as a plumber.

ANDY TILLSON

Andy Tillson must have wondered what he'd let himself in for when he arrived at Bristol Rovers. No sooner had he played his first game for The Pirates – a 5-1 defeat at Wolves – than the manager (Denis Rofe) was on his way, and over the next five months he played under three more managers – Malcolm Allison, Steve Cross and John Ward.

It says much for the genial 6ft 2in defender that despite the mind-boggling management merry-go-round taking place, Andy went on to establish himself in the heart of the Rovers defence, clocking up 300 games (including four as sub) over an eight-year period. During that time he earned the respect of fans, teammates and opposing players alike. In fact, for much of his time in Rovers' blue and white, he was club captain.

Recommended to Rovers by QPR boss Gerry Francis, Andy got the opportunity to play League football when Alan Buckley became manager at Grimsby Town. 'Alan was the single biggest influence in my career and I owe him a great deal,' said Andy. 'I'd played for him at non-League Kettering and when he moved on to Grimsby, he signed me and gave me my big chance.'

After over 100 games for The Mariners, during which time Andy played a major role in the team getting promotion twice, he got his chance to taste the big time when Queens Park Rangers paid Grimsby £400,000 for his services. 'One of my fondest memories of that time is going to Anfield and beating Liverpool 3-1,' he recalled. He later returned for a short loan spell at Grimsby before, in November 1992, Rovers paid a record transfer fee of £370,000 to bring him to Bristol.

'I've got lots of good memories of Rovers. In particular, of the fans – they took to me straight away and, as supporters go, they're different class.' But there were also disappointments for Andy. 'Losing at Wembley in the play-off final against Huddersfield was hard to take,' he admitted.

Another disappointment was Rovers' failure to make the play-offs at the end of the 1999/2000 season, after leading the division for so long. The team was broken up and, to the surprise of many true blue supporters, Andy was released to join Walsall. If proof was needed that Rovers had got it wrong, Andy led Walsall to promotion, while Rovers were relegated. Although thirty-four years old, he went on to make 52 senior appearances for the Midland side, before winding up his League career with Rushden & Diamonds.

Like many professional footballers who come to one of the Bristol clubs, Andy put his roots down in the area, living in the Bathwick area of Bath. Three years ago, he joined university-based Southern League side Team Bath and has been coaching the young players there for the past two years. He took on the role of head coach last summer.

Married to Kelly, the couple have a teenage daughter, Danielle, and a teenage son, Jordan, who is on schoolboy forms with Rovers.

Left: Andy Tillson, in his Bristol Rovers days.

Below: Ready for a coaching session with Team Bath.

MIKE TROUGHT

Mike Trought is obviously a player who can rise to the big occasion. He made his League debut away to Manchester City, marking the likes of Shaun Goater and Gareth Taylor. Later he was one of the Rovers stars who claimed the scalp of (then) top-flight side Derby County, a side that included Fabrizio Ravenelli and Benito Carbone, in an FA Cup match at Pride Park. 'I remember both games well,' said Mike. 'A nil-nil at Maine Road was an excellent result and to win 3-1 at Derby was even better.'

Although Mike made his League debut at Manchester, he'd actually made a senior appearance before then. 'That was against Walsall in an Auto Windshields cup match at The Mem and I think I'm right in saying we lost on penalties,' he recalled.

Mike had joined Rovers as a schoolboy, working his way up from the ranks. After making his Maine Road debut in December 1996, he was to spend much of his time on the bench, due to the form of central defenders Andy Tillson and Steve Foster. A loan spell at non-League Clevedon Town followed in December 2000, before he returned to Rovers, where he made 17 League starts the following season. But Mike had a run of bad luck with injuries and he was released by Ray Graydon in 2002:

> I think I played around fifty games in the first team, but injuries and a change of manager didn't help my cause, although I'll always be grateful to Ollie (Ian Holloway) and Gerry Francis for the help and advice they gave me during their time in charge.

A trial with Bournemouth looked promising, but the South Coast club was going through a financial crisis and nothing came of it. Next stop was Bath City, where Mike spent three years. But a bad injury in an FA Trophy match at Canvey Island put Mike back out of the game again. 'I fractured my knee cap and had to have an operation on it, which kept me out of football for ten months,' he revealed.

Last season Mike made another comeback, this time back at Clevedon Town as they swept all before them to win the championship of Division One (West) of the Southern League. 'The manager there is Phil Bater and he had been my youth team manager at Rovers so it was nice to play for him again,' stated Mike. 'Also, it's been great after all the setbacks to be back on the pitch playing soccer.'

A self-employed carpenter, Mike lives in Ashton with his partner Lindsay.

Left: Mike in his Rovers days.

Below: Mike at work today.

GEOFF TWENTYMAN

'As a player I'd always enjoyed giving interviews to the media, so when my playing days were nearly over and I had to consider my future, I thought, why not be on the other side of the microphone.' And that is how former Bristol Rovers centre half Geoff Twentyman explains his move to the world of sports reporting at Radio Bristol. He also has a column in the local paper.

Geoff's footballing career began at Liverpool, where he followed in the footsteps of his father, Geoff senior. Unable to get into the first team, Geoff moved into non-League football and was spotted playing for Chorley in the Northern Premier League by a Preston North End scout:

Although I played in defence, I managed to get 23 goals in one season for them. Whether Preston thought they were going to get a free-scoring central defender I don't know, but I only got one goal for them in my first season!

Geoff went on to play 110 senior games for The Lilywhites, having served under six managers during his three years there. It was one of those former managers – ex-Manchester United forward Brian Kidd – who recommended him to Bristol Rovers, after Geoff had been given a free transfer in 1986:

I signed for Rovers thinking it would be good to play at Eastville Stadium. What (manager) Bobby Gould had neglected to tell me was that the club was having to move out of their stadium and play their home games at Bath City's ground! That was typical Bobby Gould.

For the next seven years, Geoff was to be the kingpin of Rovers' defence, with teams dreading coming to the small compact ground at Twerton Park. 'I had some wonderful times with Rovers and my best memory has to be of us winning three-nil at Blackpool to win the championship,' recalls Geoff.

Geoff was to play all 46 games that season and by the time his footballing days were coming to an end he had clocked up well over 300 senior appearances for The Pirates. He could have been forgiven for thinking his days at Rovers were over when he moved into sports journalism – but they weren't. Ten months later, and with a secure job at the BBC under his belt, Geoff got a call from the (then) Rovers manager Ian 'Ollie' Holloway, who wanted him as his assistant. 'I couldn't resist it,' he admits. 'Having said that, it simply didn't work out. People were saying I'd fallen out with Ollie, but that's just not true – it simply didn't work out.'

Fortunately for Geoff he was able to return to his old job at 'the Beeb' and is a regular voice down the sports airwaves. On the domestic front he has been married to Debbie, and they have a teenage son and daughter.

Right: Geoff in action for Rovers.

Below: Ready for another radio phone-in.

JOSSER WATLING

It's common knowledge that every club has a joker in its midst, and John 'Josser' Watling didn't earn his nickname for nothing. 'A great guy, but you had to be careful you weren't the victim of one of his practical jokes,' summed up one former teammate. Mind you, if the Germans had had their way, Able Seaman John 'Josser' Watling would never have become an Eastville favourite.

'We were on convoy duty and got sunk just outside a Russian port,' Josser explained. 'Luckily we were able to transfer to another ship before she went down. Hell of a waste, it was a brand new corvette!' And that sums up the affable Bristolian, always likely to see the funny side and bring a smile to the faces of others.

Josser's Rovers career began in the 1945/46 season, when he signed amateur forms for the club, having been spotted playing for Avonmouth St Andrews. He made his debut for the first team in the 1947/48 season, finishing up on the losing side in a 5-1 defeat to arch rivals Bristol City. That was the first of 354 senior games spanning fifteen years in Rovers' blue and white quarters. 'I think our best side was probably in the 1950/51 season,' he reflected. 'That was a great team with a one-for-all and all-for-one attitude.'

Not the fastest of wingers, Josser made up for that with a shimmy that would often leave the opposing defender tackling thin air. He also had an uncanny knack of being able to float in inch-perfect centres for the likes of Geoff Bradford and Vic Lambden.

'Alfie Biggs was another great forward,' said Josser. But wasn't it Josser who came up with Alfie's nickname The Baron? 'Yes, that was down to me,' admitted Josser. 'You see, Alfie was always immaculately dressed and never short of a bob or two, so calling him The Baron seemed about right!'

Josser missed out on qualifying for a medal after losing his place in the side that played most of the games in the 1952/53 promotion season, although manager Bert Tann had no hesitation in recalling the winger when the team hit a wobble towards the end of the campaign. And the move up to the Second Division seemed to bring out the best in him.

As the years went by, a new young prospect with a cannonball shot, Peter Hooper, was a serious threat to Josser's place in the side. Manager Bert Tann's answer was to switch Josser to left-back and play them both. Taking to the role like a duck to water, he went on to complete 354 senior appearances, scored 21 goals and took on the role of club captain, before retiring from professional football in 1962.

After soccer, Josser ran a fruit shop for two years and then worked as a storekeeper at Glenside Hospital, retiring eighteen years later.

Married to Maureen (his first wife Helen died in 1978), Josser lives just down the road from Rovers' old Eastville home. He has two children, five grandchildren and one great-grandchild.

Opposite above: A 1950s Rovers line-up, with Josser in the front row, far right.

Opposite below: 'That was me,' says Josser.

IAN WESTON

'We've certainly come a long way since the days of the bucket and sponge.' That's the verdict of former Rovers player Ian Weston, who like former Rovers goalkeeper Phil Kite, is a qualified physiotherapist.

A full-back or midfield player, Ian joined The Pirates as an apprentice in 1984, signing full-time professional forms two years later:

> I remember making my senior debut as an eighteen-year-old in an FA Cup match at Brentford and they had a really tricky winger called Andy Sinton. I got booked after just ten minutes and sent off early in the second half. Sinton was good – too good for me that day!

Brentford won the tie 2-0, but Ian had the satisfaction of going back there the same month to make his League debut and, having learnt from the first game, helped his team to a 2-1 victory.

Four years on and Ian moved down the road to Torquay United. 'The highlight of my time there was playing at Wembley in the Leyland Daf final,' said Ian. 'The late Cyril Knowles was manager and we beat Rovers on our way to Wembley.' Although Torquay lost 4-1 to Bolton in that final, Ian relished the chance to play on Wembley's hallowed turf. 'A fantastic experience,' he summed up.

As well as two seasons at Torquay, Ian had a loan spell with Shamrock Rovers, before stepping down to non-League football with Bath City. 'I had four years at Bath and was in the side that knocked Cardiff City out of the FA Cup at Ninian Park.' Ian also had two loan spells at Cheltenham Town, who are his current employers.

After Bath, Ian turned out for Clevedon Town, but a troublesome knee injury ended his playing days:

> I decided I wanted to stay in the game as a physiotherapist and, as well as studying for my qualifications, I was lucky that Clevedon gave me the chance of hands-on experience. I moved on to Forest Green, before getting the chance to be physiotherapist at Cheltenham, which is where I am now. The thing about physiotherapy is that you never stop learning. Things have moved on a lot from the old days. Players take a lot more care and interest about their health and their diet, and fitness levels are constantly monitored.

Ian is one of three former Rovers players at Cheltenham, which is just forty-five minutes from his home in Kingswood. Bob Bloomer is in charge of the youth academy and former Rovers (and City) boss John Ward is the manager.

Married to Sam, the couple have a young son, Joseph, and daughter, Alexandra.

Opposite above: Ian (second right) in his Torquay days, tackling Exeter's Steve Neville.

Opposite below: Ian is now the physiotherapist at Cheltenham Town.

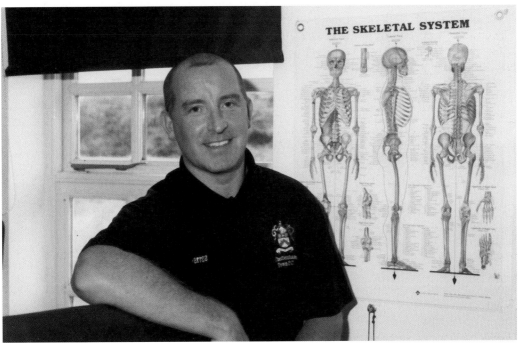

DEVON WHITE

Back in 1987, Rovers manager Gerry Francis was looking for someone to add that extra 'spark' to his attack. He remembered a big gangly centre forward he'd come across and found that the 6ft-plus striker had left League football to concentrate on being an electrician. Who better to add that missing 'spark' than big Devon White?

Devon had started a League career at Lincoln City in 1984, scoring four times in 29 appearances:

> The club had been relegated and my contract was up, so I thought that was the end of that, as far as League football was concerned. I'd had a loan spell at Boston United and had qualified as an electrician, so I'd accepted that a career as a professional footballer was probably not going to happen.

Shortly after joining The Pirates, Devon found himself thrust in at the deep end with a first-team opportunity which he grabbed with both hands. 'We were due to play Aldershot at Twerton Park and Rovers striker Robbie Turner had got delayed coming over from Cardiff and so Gerry told me I was in.' It was a dream start for Devon, who scored one of Rovers' first-half goals and kept his place in the side, scoring in the next two games for them.

Having formed a deadly partnership with the tricky Gary Penrice, Rovers fans immediately took to the striker, giving him the nickname 'Bruno' because of his likeness to boxer Frank Bruno. Terrace chants of 'Bru-no, Bru-no' were soon echoing round the ground, as he delighted Rovers fans with his total commitment to the cause.

Over the course of the next five seasons, Devon notched up 228 (plus 12 as sub) appearances. His 60 goals for the club included two against arch rivals Bristol City to clinch promotion from the Third Division and the consolation goal at Wembley, when Rovers lost 2-1 to Tranmere in the Leyland Daf final.

Fans were surprised when Rovers let him go to Cambridge United in 1992, as part of the deal that brought John Taylor to the club, but when Gerry Francis, by then managing Queens Park Rangers in the top flight, decided he needed a big bustling striker, he was once again looking up Devon's phone number:

> What Gerry achieved at Rovers and then QPR was nothing short of a miracle. Money was practically non-existent at Rovers, but he took us up and got us to the Daf cup final. Then, on very limited resources, he turned Rangers into one of London's top clubs.

After 26 games and nine goals for Rangers, Devon moved on, playing for Notts County, Watford, Notts County again and finally Shrewsbury Town, before leaving League football in 1999 and playing part-time for Ilkeston Town in the Northern Premier League.

Now living back in his native Nottingham, Devon looks back on his time with Rovers with great fondness. 'Things went better than I could possibly have dreamed,' he summed up. 'The club, the fans, what can I say... absolutely fantastic.'

Devon (second left) receives the congratulations of teammates Phil Purnell and David Mehew, after scoring for Rovers at Wembley.

Devon White today, on a return visit to Rovers.

STEVE WHITE

If anyone has any doubts that practice, dedication and sheer hard work have their own rewards, they could do worse than have a chat with Steve White. The fact that the former Rovers striker was still playing in the Football League while in his late thirties and scored 232 goals in over 650 games is proof enough. 'I've always worked very hard at improving my game,' said Steve. 'Also, I was very lucky in that I never had any serious injuries during my career.'

Steve joined Bristol Rovers in 1977, replacing local hero Paul Randall, who had moved on to the top flight at Stoke City. A return of 20 goals from 46 games alerted Luton Town, who paid out just under £200,000 to take him to Kenilworth Road. 'David Pleat was the manager there and he steered the team to winning the old Second Division championship,' recalled Steve.

A part-exchange deal saw Steve move on to Charlton Athletic, with Paul Walsh moving in the opposite direction. 'A well run club,' was Steve's verdict on Athletic, who had a certain Lennie Lawrence as club coach at the time.

During his time at Charlton – 29 starts and 12 goals – Steve had loan spells at Lincoln City and his old club Luton, before Rovers boss David Williams brought him back home in August 1983. After three years in his second spell with The Pirates, Williams' successor, Bobby Gould, released Steve, who signed for Swindon Town.

'Bobby Gould letting me go was the best thing he ever did for me!' said Steve, with a smile. Swindon, under the astute management of Lou Macari, was the perfect platform for Steve's skills, and in his eight years at The County Ground he netted 83 times in 244 games.

'We got to the play-off finals twice – the first time beating Sunderland to go up to the top flight,' said Steve. But celebrations were cut short when the team was denied promotion, following an investigation into financial irregularities at the club. 'That was a real body blow, but we returned three years later under Ossie Ardiles to beat Leicester in a seven-goal thriller and go up into the old First Division,' Steve pointed out.

After his successful time at Swindon, Steve moved on to Hereford United (44 goals, 76 games) and finished his League career at Cardiff City, where he scored 15 times in 67 games.

A spell as assistant manager to former Swindon teammate Paul Bodin at Bath City followed and, more recently, he had eighteen months at Southern League side Chippenham Town, where he was the most successful manager in the club's history.

Married to Mandy, the couple live in picturesque Old Sodbury. They have a daughter, Ashley, whose sporting passion is horses and son Joseph, who is showing promise reminiscent of his dad as a teenage striker.

Left: Former Pirate Steve White on the ball.

Below: Steve White today.

TOM WHITE

For a player that made a few moves in his career, it shouldn't come as too much of a surprise to learn that former Rovers defender Tom White now helps others with moves of their own – he's the manager of an estate agents in Bedminster.

Prior to helping people with their 'comings and goings', Tom had started off a football career with Rovers. 'I joined the club straight from school, when Tony Gill was youth team manager,' said Tom when we met up at his place of work. Signing as a full-time professional in 1994, Tom made his senior debut the following year. 'I had a run in the first team but then went down with glandular fever, which set me back a fair time,' he said.

It was to be nineteen months before Tom got back into the side, but between 1996 and 1998 he made a strong claim for the central defensive position, during which time he notched up his only League goal, in a 3-2 defeat at Watford. In 1999 he had a short loan spell at Kingstonian, before being loaned to Hereford United, where he made 16 appearances. 'When I went back to Rovers my contract was up. I wanted first-team football, which Rovers couldn't guarantee and after discussing the situation with Ollie (manager Ian Holloway) I left the club,' he explained.

So, having made over fifty appearances for The Pirates, Tom headed north for a trial period with Carlisle United, but that didn't work out. 'Ian Atkins was the manager there at the time and let's just say we didn't have the same ideas of how football should be played, so I left,' he revealed.

The chance to join Yeovil Town, under Dave Webb proved to be a better option for Tom:

> Yeovil had just gone full-time as they set about getting into the Football League and I stayed there for three seasons, first under Dave Webb and later Gary Johnson. They had a great team spirit and I enjoyed my time there, although you had to watch out for the club's practical joker, Terry Skiverton.

Tom went on to play over sixty games for The Glovers and also had a short loan spell at Woking. Then, another loan move, this time to Tiverton to regain fitness, went disastrously wrong:

> I'd suffered a knee injury at Yeovil and went out on loan to Tiverton in order to get match fit. That was a disaster as I damaged ligaments in my right leg in my first game. The end result was I had an operation to have the knee realigned, was sidelined for a year-and-a-half and after that full-time football was out of the question.

After leaving full-time football, Tom has played for Mangotsfield United in the Southern Premier League, although his work at the estate agents takes priority as Saturdays are one of their busiest days. Tom lives in Kingswood with his partner Louise and young son Zachary.

Left: Tom in his Bristol Rovers days.

Below: Looking after a client at the estate agents.

MIKE WYATT

When Mike Wyatt started off on soccer's rocky road, the only thing he had designs on was a long and successful career as a professional footballer. Sadly, after just a handful of games for both City and Rovers, he was one of the many young pros who found themselves surplus to requirements and went for a career outside the game. He's still got designs though – he's a graphic designer for a local newspaper! 'Obviously it was a disappointment to come out of the game, but I think you realise that it may happen and you just have to get on with life,' said Mike.

Born in Yate, Mike had a two-year apprenticeship at City in the early 1990s and went on to make his debut in a 3-1 defeat at Wolverhampton Wanderers. 'Russell Osman was the manager at the time,' said Mike. 'He's played the game at the highest level, so he knows what it's all about, and he gave me my big chance, for which I shall always be grateful.'

Mike went on to make a dozen or so appearances for the first team, before new manager Joe Jordan decided Mike wasn't part of his future plans. 'I'd had a few injuries, which didn't help, and Joe decided to let me go,' said Mike philosophically.

Having been released by City, Mike had a big decision to make. He had the choice of moving north to one of the Scottish clubs, an offer to join the soccer exodus to Hong Kong or go to Bristol Rovers! 'I didn't really fancy moving away and Terry Connor, who had been at City during my time there, was one of Rovers' coaches, which probably swayed it for me,' explained Mike.

Despite a promising start with The Pirates, Mike's career there never really took off and after one season and another handful of games, he once again had to make decisions about his future. 'I did enjoy my time with Rovers, although it never really happened for me there,' he said. 'John Ward was the manager and although he was the one to let me go, I've got the utmost respect for the man.'

Not that Mike needed to travel far for his next club, signing on for non-League Bath City. 'I had three years at Bath but, conscious of the need to get a trade behind me, I went to college to study graphic design,' he said.

He moved on from Bath to join Gloucester City, where he spent two-and-a-half years, followed by a season at Worcester. After that, he got the call to return to Twerton Park. 'To be honest, going back to Bath didn't work out,' he admitted. 'I never really got on with the manager and I don't think he'd ever seen me play before, so why he signed me is a mystery.'

Staying with the local non-League scene, Mike had just over two seasons with Clevedon Town and is currently enjoying his fourth season with Yate Town in the Southern League.

Married to Claire, the couple live in the Yate area with their young daughter Tilly.

Left: Mike in his Rovers days.

Below: Mike Wyatt today.

Other titles published by STADIA

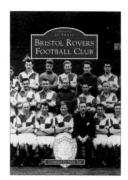

Bristol Rovers Football Club
MIKE JAY

This pictorial selection traces the fortunes of Rovers from the Eastville Stadium to the Memorial Ground, featuring promotion seasons, epic cup runs and some famous victories over the other team in Bristol. Many of the important characters from the past are included: Bert Tann, Don Megson and Gerry Francis; Geoff Bradford, Harold Jarman, Alan Warboys and Gary Mabbutt. This is an essential read for all loyal Gasheads.
0 7524 1150 0

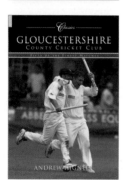

Speedway in Bristol 1928-1949
ROBERT BAMFORD & JOHN JARVIS

Speedway first came to Bristol in 1928 at the Knowle Stadium. The first period of racing came to an end in 1930, but the sport returned in 1936, when the club acquired the nickname 'Bulldogs'. For a while Bristol were the best supported team in the Provincial League, also spending a season in the top division before the war. After hostilities ceased, another terrific promotion to Division One was achieved in 1949. This is the definitive history of Bristol Speedway up to that time.

0 7524 3788 7

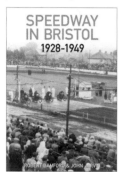

Gloucestershire CCC Classic Matches
ANDREW HIGNELL

Gloucestershire CCC has had no shortage of exciting and significant matches over the years. Since the days of the great Dr W.G. Grace, many illustrious players have graced the county grounds and entertained the crowds with their exploits. This selection aims to present the fifty most significant first-class matches in terms of the history of the county. The text is accompanied by many wonderful illustrations and a scorecard is included for each match.
0 7524 3212 5

Barrie Meyer Getting It Right
BARRIE MEYER WITH ANDREW HIGNELL

Barrie Meyer has had a lifetime in professional sport, as a cricketer with Gloucestershire, a footballer with Bristol Rovers and City (amongst others) and twenty-five years as a first-class and Test match umpire. His memorable moments as a footballer include being part of the Rovers side that beat Manchester United in the 1956 FA Cup and his cricketing anecdotes about the likes of Ian Botham, Viv Richards, Dickie Bird and Curtly Ambrose make this a hugely entertaining read.
0 7524 4007 1

If you are interested in purchasing other books published by Stadia, or in case you have difficulty finding any Stadia books in your local bookshop, you can also place orders directly through the Tempus Publishing website
www.tempus-publishing.com